B17 949

Pacific off
univ.

# CRYSTAL MIRROR

VOLUME III

*Crystal Mirror* is the annual journal of the Tibetan Nyingma Meditation Center, 2425 Hillside Ave., Berkeley, Calif. 94704

Copyright © 1974 Dharma Publishing, 5856 Doyle St., Emeryville, Calif. 94608

Typography and Printing by Dharma Press

International Standard Book Number: 0–913546–05–4

Printed in the United States of America

Frontispiece: The Lotus-Born Guru Padma Sambhava

# A Word from Tarthang Tulku,

TIBET, MY HOMELAND, was a beautiful country—not only because of the natural beauty of its land, but because of the emphasis on a simple, meaningful way of life. The atmosphere was very supportive of people who wished to devote their time to spiritual practice.

Now that I have lived here in America for some years, I can feel people truly questioning the very essence of life. Inner development and clarity are more and more becoming the purpose of everyday life. If people can become more harmoniously balanced and feel positive, then this is something very useful, especially in America.

Literally, Buddha's teachings are for everyone. The teachings go beyond cultural boundaries and touch the root of each human being's consciousness. How our minds evolve can either be healthy or self-destructive. Each moment we have the opportunity to find satisfaction within.

Ten years ago, Tibetan Buddhism was almost unheard of, and now many people, young and old, have heard of Tibet. For some, the deepest revelation of their lives has been to follow the Dharma, and this gives them a positive path. The disciplines and practices of the Teachings have unquestionable results, and this is difficult to ignore. All sentient beings want peace and happiness, and I think the Dharma can help people realize this.

My tradition is the Nyingma, and, of course, I whole-heartedly believe in the effectiveness of this path. I hope that anyone who feels he has found an easier method to reach enlightenment is not disillusioned. Generally our ordinary mind finds satisfaction in the very tricks and subtleties that cause us suffering. Our minds create the world of our experience, but we are very small, and our minds are very small. We cannot completely trust this mind.

Buddhism has many levels of teachings which each sentient being can understand according to his mental development. Vajrayana is a very unique method of shortening the way to enlightenment. All that would normally be shunned or overlooked—such as strong emotions, desires, or confusions—are seen as valuable tools. But this Vajrayana path necessarily involves complete openness to each experience, and the willingness to investigate thoroughly the causes of dissatisfaction.

At times we may become discouraged with our failings, but this too is another teaching. We need to encourage each other—our friends and relatives, whoever we come in contact with—so that they may find inspiration in the positive attitude of the Dharma, without too many speculations or confusions.

We may have different styles to express ourselves, but ultimately we are very much one with the people of the world. We are born and we shall die, and each shall reap the harvest of his past actions. This life will pass like a rainbow in the sky, all too quickly gone—while the precious chance of this life is to find self-realization.

This past year has been very full and many wonderful people have come to share our goals and contribute to the Center's development. We are very grateful. May the Gurus of the precious lineage of Padma Sambhava, the Lotus-Born, remove all obscurations and hindrances, and shower each one of you with love and compassion for all sentient beings.

With the blessings of the Triple Gem,

Tarthang Tulku, Rinpoche
Head Lama of the Tibetan
Nyingma Meditation Center

# CRYSTAL MIRROR

## VOLUME III

PART ONE

# TEACHINGS

# Mind is the Root

*Praise to the Jnanasattva Manjushri*
*who is none else but one's mind*
*one with the Guru*

M IND IS THE ROOT *of both Samsara and Nirvana:*
*There is no entity of reality that has not sprung from mind.*
*The frolicking and dancing of worldly and transworldly apparitions*
 *in all their multiplicity*
*Comes to an end when its creator, mind as a magician,*
 *has been overpowered.*

*Non-understanding is the mind gone astray into any*
 *of its six kinds of existences;*
*Understanding this mind is 'pristine awareness.'*
*Pristine awareness is Buddhahood, and*
*As the quintessence of happiness it resides in one's heart.*

### *Hum*    OM AH HUM

---

LAMA MI-PHAM [Mi-pham 'Jam-dbYang rNam-rGyal rGya-mTso, "The Completely Victorious Ocean of Gentle Voice"] was an incarnation of Manjushri, and the most renowned and comprehensive scholar in Tibet during the 19th century.

Lama Mi-pham systematized the sutras and philosophical tantras, and wrote 32 volumes, including works on music, logic, astrology, alchemy, and medicine. He compiled and practiced over 200 sadhanas, and at one time spent 7 years in retreat. He taught at Katog, Dzog-chen, and Zhe-chen as well as other great monasteries in Eastern Tibet [Kham]. He carries on the direct lineage of Pal-trul Rinpoche, Jam Yang Khyentse Wangpo, and Jam Gon Kongtrul.

*Look this way, look at your mind:*
*Wide are the eyes that look at everything everywhere,*
*Like a beloved child with whom one has long been together.*
*What is seen compared to what is said to be 'my mind'?*
*Now is the time to look at this 'my mind':*
*Better it is to take a profound look within*
*Than letting the eyes roam over the external realms.*


*Even if one were to enter the pristine awareness*
        *in which there is no duality*
*And which has one flavor, in its intrinsicness,*
        *when one has realized*
*That all the entities of reality are ineffable*
        *in their apparitionalness,*
*It is by this looking at one's mind that in one moment*
        *and in one big sweep*
*One tears open the hidden recesses of the mind*
        *craving what appears before it*
*And sees the very core of pristine cognitiveness.*
*Therefore this is called the 'short cut.'*
*There is no need to unite technique and discrimination*
        *in what is the unity of the aesthetic continuum*
        *and its intrinsic awareness.*
*The fact that this continuum and its awareness are not such that*
        *they can be added to or abstracted from each other*
*Has been laid bare, O fortunate seeker.*

A–HO     [OPENNESS AND BLISS]


*The appearance of a world of objects is the frolicking of the mind;*
*If there is no mind, who knows the objects?*
*This very act of knowing is not something apart from the mind:*
*While there is nothing, there is yet appearance and this is the*
        *self-presentation of apparitionalness.*

A–HO


*This mind has nothing about it that could allow it*
        *to be taken hold of;*
*If it had, one could concentrate on what is already there;*
*If not, one would concentrate on something non-existent.*
*Do not disrupt unity into such opposites.*

A–HO

*That which is not-two, dispels (the idea of) duality;*
*That which is not definable as one, appears as a duality.*
*That which cannot be objectified as 'this,'*
*Is the self-settledness of the King, Mind-as-such.*

A–Ho

*Even if one does not know what to concentrate upon*
*But by seeing it as unattainable, though not*
*In the manner of having thrown something away or lost,*
*Is to have come to the foundations of mind.*
*Let this attainment be in the realm of the unattainable.*
*Once you let it be there,*
*Although there is no longer any concrete entity,*
*You have the creativeness of the all-illumining cognitiveness.*

*The aesthetic continuum and the intrinsic awareness*
        *which are not two entities, are such that none*
        *can be added to or subtracted from the other.*
*In this nothingness they have no essence of nothingness;*
*If investigated they are nothing as such, but if let alone*
        *they shine in a primal light.*
*They are not caught by grasping for them, but are like*
        *the moon's reflection in the water.*
*Devoid of any essence such as cause, effect, presence,*
        *coming-and-going,*
*The actuality of this openness is a self-existent iridescence.*
*The response of and to this luminosity never ceases,*
*How can it be soiled by contradictions and arguments*
        *concerned with non-existence or existence!*

*In investigating mind, mind is an analogy for pristine awareness:*
*In understanding it, it is the self-present intrinsicness*
        *in pristine awareness.*
*What a miracle!—This effulgence of mind in Mind-as-such.*

*What is its use in being open, what point is there*
        *in its appearing?*
*Who is this in which there is no duality, what is it*
        *that is to be concentrated upon?*
*Preserve it as what it is in its self-settledness.*

*According to their various capacities, individuals*
*See this pristine awareness that is beyond the ordinary mind*
*Either gradually or, at their best, at once.*

*In this pristine awareness yogis burn the seeds*
  *of the six kinds of existence*
  *together with their potentialities*
*By the fires of the indestructible nature of reality,*
  *that come as the embodiment, communication, and*
  *appreciation of values,*
*That are the self-creativeness of the pristine awareness*
  *in one's heart;*
*Out of their innermost being the sun of infinite strength and*
  *indestructible confidence shines forth.*
*They hold this pristine awareness with folded hands,*
*And in a single lifetime reach primordial Buddhahood.*

SAMAYA

I wrote these verses
when I was meditating on Heruka
on the 15th day of the 11th month of the iron-horse year
and felt like an old dog whose teeth
and the bone in its mouth had seemed to become one
and suddenly were vomited.
Or, when love filled a young man, glancing and swaggering around,
whilst meeting a beautiful girl, adorned in her finery —
then words came genuinely and spontaneously. ❖

# On Thoughts

*If wandering thoughts keep on arising,*
*Catch hold of your Self-mind with alertness.*
*Be attached not to Samsara nor Nirvana,*
*But rest yourself at ease in full Equality.*
*Let what arises rise,*
*Take care not to follow.*

MILAREPA

As soon as we start to say something, meditation is destroyed. As soon as we start to conceptualize, at that moment, the meditation experience runs away. And yet, without saying something, without examining, it doesn't seem satisfying. So, to feel that we understand, we use verbal symbols. That is our nature—we use words to express things, to give measurement: it's like this, or like that. We have ideas: it's not like this, it's not like that. But, finally we become blocked. We can't express real meaning so we become frustrated. We think that we can't know something unless we can measure it. But really, the only simple way is to go directly into the situation, to see it, be it, and then express it. Then, some sort of 'understanding,' or 'experience,' may come through this very narrow channel.

So how do we break this shell of conception? How can we crack our own thoughts? This shell is like gravity, and thoughts in a way have gravity. They pull with tremendous force, characteristic of our dual

*cracking*
*our*
*thoughts*

TARTHANG TULKU RINPOCHE, is a reincarnate lama of Tarthang Monastery in Eastern Tibet. He carries on the Dzog-chen Nying-tig lineage of the Nyingma school which traces its origin through Padma Sambhava to Lord Buddha. Articles by Tarthang Tulku are edited transcriptions of talks given in early 1974.

mind. On the surface of the ocean there are many vibrations, many heavy waves. But if you go down just twenty feet, it's very quiet, very calm, very still. It's the same with our minds. In the outer form of one thought, the forces are very active. Go further in and there is stillness . . . you can find it in the thought. There is no distraction left.

In meditation we try to find a different consciousness than our usual state of mind. Our mind or thoughts are always running here and there, rapidly changing. We cannot still or relax our mind, and so we cannot focus on it.

Basically, there are two ways to approach the mind. One is intellectual: we examine and analyze it. Forget these things. Concepts have limits. We want to try to deal with mind and thought directly. One approach is to try to scare away all thoughts, or maybe tranquilize them so that meditation becomes a big vastness: no thoughts, no concepts, very peaceful, very still.

In another way, it's possible to make the thought itself meditation. Most of the time, our problems are really thoughts—our emotions and judgments make us disturbed. But the substance of thought itself can become meditation. As thoughts come, limitations, fixations and judgments are set up. But if our awareness is in the center of thought, the thought itself dissolves. The mind is completely aware, completely balanced. *make the thought itself meditation*

How do we go into that state? The moment you try to separate yourself from thought, you are dealing with duality, a subject-object relationship. You lose the state of awareness because you reject your experience and become separate from it. You are trying to catch a rainbow: it seems close, and at the same time you can't reach it. Mind is sensitive, like radar, dividing reality into hundredths of seconds. It always needs relationships, objects, this and that. It needs something to touch, and cannot survive alone. But there is a way to go into true stillness, where no one is holding, where no one is preparing meditation, where no one is left out. This state is all inclusive: nothing is left other than meditation or, you could say, complete awareness, complete dance.

With any kind of thought, or form, you have mental activities going on. Before the conceptualization, you can be in the thought and you can stay in it . . . within the moment, within that very first state. At the very beginning, almost nothing moves. Stay in the concepts, the thoughts. Just be there. You can do this, and it automatically becomes meditation, automatically becomes balance, automatically becomes awareness. There is no need for any support, or knowledge, or any instructions, or anybody. There is no outside 'you' left. You become the center of the thought. But there is not really any center—the center becomes balance. There's no 'being,' no 'object-subject relationships': *just be there* none of these categories exist. Yet at the same time, there is functionality, there is complete openness.

*within thought*

The beauty of your own nature allows you to exercise upon these things: within thought, within concepts. First, a thought comes: okay, I see it . . . and thought may sometimes hypnotize me completely, so that I completely swallow it: I become the thought. But then, sometimes, the thought may not completely block me, and I can see it, but I cannot get free. The thoughts are there, always pulling me back. Sometimes, thoughts pull at your legs: you have no free access, no liberation . . . you are not free, you're tied up. Or sometimes, thoughts build a wall: you can't see anything other than that thought. Sometimes I myself become the thought. *I am the thought.* It seems we have little control over our own thoughts.

The one who is practicing, the meditator, is trying to see: "A thought is coming . . . now it's coming, be careful." You try to push it back . . . it goes back and forth. Sometimes you win, sometimes you lose. But we don't realize *who he is* that is pushing: that's another kind of thought manifestation. Your own mind is making tricks. Who is pushing?—that's another kind of thought. And then it's back and forth again, pulling and pushing. It takes a long time to realize that all of this is a game.

*mind games*

A very wise person, who has great experience, will later on realize that all of it's a game . . . tricks. You're playing mind games, many inner dialogues. Later on you realize how you've been wasting time. For many years of meditation you've been doing things perfectly, giving lots of effort—but, you know, it's a waste of time, of no value. You don't realize that it's always the thought's game—making your own self-tricks. So gradually we become old. Children are so fascinated by their own games, but then they become older and wiser, and, though they still enjoy them, they know they're not truly real. In the same way, as you find maturity in your own practice, you see that all this pushing and pulling, all these games, are the same family. There's no differences.

Soon you become less interested in these games. Thoughts come, or they don't come . . . emotions come, or they don't come . . . and you do not become so fixated by them. As you mature, you develop a big mind. You don't care so much. Your mind becomes less narrow. If you become skillful, you can go *into* that thought—into the front of it, or into the back of it, or into the one that is making the judgments about it: "This is good . . . this is not good." Maybe you can embrace that judgmental one who is you trying to discriminate, "This is not good." You may embrace your judging mind and become united with it.

*embrace the judgmental mind*

So we kind of crack each thought, like cracking nuts. If we can do this, any thought becomes meditation. Any mental activities, any situation, can be transcended into that state of balance. Negative characteristics are lost and transcended into a form of meditation. At that time, they no longer exist as ordinary mind, or samsaric mind. Ordinary consciousness already will have been transformed, but it's kind of paradoxical . . . how it happens is very subtle. As soon as you try to do something, immediately it is a 'second state'—the next thought, or second state of mind. Mind changes so quickly. So you need to very carefully develop 'skillful means.'

Trying hard is not effective in meditation. But be confident and don't try to mold your practice into a perfect pattern: "Oh, this is not concentration . . . this is not the right way . . . this may be something else." Don't use the energy conceptually, giving it names, always expressing yourself to yourself. Forget about concepts. Get away from trying to identify—"Is this wisdom? or awareness? or meditation? or God-consciousness? or this or that?" Don't try to make anything. You don't need to worry about whether this is good or bad or right or wrong. All these things are judgments. Don't worry and don't give power to judgments. Just forget it, absolutely forget it. Just be *in* there following your own kind of openness, at any thought, any time. There is no special time. Any time there is a thought or activity—just be. Don't try to escape. Don't try to ignore. Don't try to do anything. Do nothing. Does that mean escaping? No—no one's escaping . . . no one's trying anything.

*don't give power to judgments*

So, become centerlessness . . . with no subject, no object, nothing in between. Don't try to do anything. The nature of reality cannot be reached by trying hard.

### The nature of mind is so subtle

At first, as you gain experience, you feel, "Ah, I can see . . . there is a place . . . I can see very subtle distinctions." Once you really find that place, it is so infinite . . . bigger than this universe. This world, this universe as we conceive it, is all included within that state of consciousness, that underlying nature. And that nature is completely centerless. In one way, everything is included, and in another way, nothing really is in it. The nature of the mind is so subtle—in one sense it is infinite, and in another sense it is very limited. In this world, whatever exists has limits—form has limits, knowledge has limits. Ordinary consciousness has limits. But from another view, there are no limits —not even the distinction between limits and limitlessness exists.

*completely centerless*

But often we may think, "Okay now, I would like to express something verbally. Conceptually, I'd like to make a model of this, to bring something out or to give information." This is part of the distraction of the individual ego. "I have discovered new things. I want to report it to me. I'm excited." This is samsaric mind: the conceptual ideas make you excited. The mind makes patterns: "This is my idea, my life, my world, my country, my culture—so many things. *I've* named it, *I've* labeled it, *I've* made up these shapes, *I* did it." But actually these are just mental discriminations, projections. What is underlying all of this? We say that all existence is made up of atoms, or of energy—or some indefinable combination of these ideas. What is our consciousness made out of? Actually, it is all the same reality, the same energy. Our consciousness or mind is made up of the infinite. In meditation, it becomes self-manifested.

*without discriminating*

But then, you don't accept this. You have problems. You cannot accept it because you think God is very high, Buddha is very high, Enlightenment is very far from you, and no one can reach Nirvana, and you are dominated by a lower person, a sinful, negative, impure person. Actually, if we look carefully, this is all discrimination. We're making blockages. Thoughts always come and interrupt, saying, "That is not possible . . . this doctrine says . . . intellectually, it could not be." You make it more difficult for yourself with so many discriminations and negative judgments. We don't accept it, and then we cannot taste it, we cannot see it. As long as we cannot taste it, we lose confidence. Then we are on the outside of Nirvana, the outside of the nature of Buddha. We can think, if Nirvana is that simple, then I am now already in Nirvana. But as soon as I *think*, then I am not in Nirvana. Even if I try to pretend, and not say anything, that doesn't help either.

We do not really know where we are or who we are. We have concepts of Nirvana, Enlightenment, God-consciousness, or Infinity, but our ideas are so restricted. Intellectually we have given everything a shape. We have civilized everything intellectually—so we can find nothing. We almost cannot think about, say, or do anything.

### Samsara and Nirvana

In Buddhism, there is only a very subtle distinction between Samsara and Nirvana. It means there aren't really any differences between the world and heaven. It's only a matter of realizing or not realizing it. And whether we realize it or not, or reach that state or not, depends on very little, because there's really no difference between the two. It's even difficult to know which side of the coin is realization and which is not realization—they're both the same coin. If one side of the coin is not there, the other side can't be there. If the front side of my hand doesn't exist, the back side cannot exist. Similarly, if this consciousness or this mind or this thought does not exist, then my meditation cannot survive.

*no difference*

That meditation, that Nirvana, is so close—there's no time and distance. We have words naming it, but it's only a word: *Nowness*.

When there is no time or distance, we call it nowness, this very moment, the presence of your mind, the presence of your thought. Ancient Buddhism has an illustration, a drawing of a circle: one part is Nirvana, one part is Samsara. The moment you can go *into* there, you are enlightened. There are many diagrams and symbolic drawings to show the practitioner how close nowness is—there is really no distance to it. In other words, we are always within it—just as we are now. We are not separated from that Reality. We're not separated from meditation. Our mind is not separate from Buddha-nature.

*no time and distance*

But due to a lack of understanding, or not-knowing, our usual thought form is clouded or deluded. We also have all kinds of conflicting emotions and negativity, which are characteristic of Samsara. Because of these obscurations we see Enlightenment as small. It doesn't seem substantial—like a soap bubble. But we have this idea because we are not *in* there. If we become the inside of the bubble, then we find infinity there. But as long as we are not in there, we feel this way or that way, always judging, because the nature of the mind is dual.

*inside the bubble*

There is a children's story about a tortoise and a frog. The tortoise comes from a distance to see the frog who lives in a very, very small lake. And they talk to each other.

"Where do you come from?"

"I come from the ocean."

"What is that?"

"It's like . . . ah . . . it's like the *ocean*."

"Can you explain to me what the ocean is? . . . Where I live, here," says the frog, "this is so big. Can you explain how big the ocean is? Is it half this size? full size?"

And the tortoise says, "More than that. The ocean is much bigger than where you live."

But the frog has only a limited experience—he cannot believe that there is anywhere bigger than his lake. There is no way to describe to him how big the ocean is.

So the tortoise brings the frog to the ocean to show him how big it is. And the frog is so astounded by the *vastness* . . . he almost faints.

We say we live in Samsara, or we live in the Kali Yuga, a time of great depression, negativity, and all kinds of problems. But even in the darkest time, the light is more bright than any other time. Even during the worst possible depression, or when the worst things happen, the light shines within a thought. You can find it . . . your true guide is there. Your true teacher, the teaching, is your own realization, and that's your real father, your guide, your teaching, your knowledge, your wisdom. You don't need to worry about your body or your thoughts . . . everything is perfect.

*your true teacher*

*everything*
*is*
*perfect*

This is not just an idea, or some kind of fantasy. Everything *is* perfect. Even though somebody breaks a leg, and has problems, and it's difficult, and wires get crossed, and there's an energy crisis, and an economic problem, and people can't get jobs, and everybody has many complaints . . . still, the essence of your own consciousness can become peace. Your head can be clear, and the world may not disturb you.

Perhaps as long as you are in a samsaric condition, you may have to face something, but, in the mind, who is working? Who is working in this world? Who created it?—our thoughts. In a way, it's like a child asking, "Who created this whole world?" We may say 'God,' or so-and-so, or *karma*—but actually, our thoughts created it.

Whatever we have in our consciousness is good 'stuff'—it's very useful. In Buddhism they talk of a 'path' . . . what is a path? what is practice? *Path, stages* . . . why do we need these things? Why do we need to practice?—because the practice is *thought*, the practice is experience. As long as there is thought, we need to practice. When there is no longer thought-form, when this is transcended, there is no path, no road—not even any goal or results. The path is only thought. When there are thought-forms, you need this path. When there are no thought-forms, there is nothing left—it has become its own reality, or, you could say, 'Thatness.' It has become reality itself.

*the path*

In a way, the path is so simple: as long as you have thought, as long as you have concepts, that's your path. There seem to be many differences, and even conflicts, in Buddhist practices and doctrines. But as long as you have thought, that's your path, that's your practice. Thought itself is practice. When you have no thoughts left, no problems, no extremes—then you are beyond the path. It means you become the absolute, the Buddha-nature.

*thought*
*itself*
*is practice*

Many people talk of happiness, or enjoyment, or satisfaction, but it's only an idea. When one day you really have it, then you know it. You're convinced. You don't even need to express how it is—the question doesn't arise. You don't necessarily have to think, "Oh, this is like that." You don't care whether somebody approves you or disproves you—you don't care too much, you're not anxious . . . you *know* it. And there's nothing higher than *knowing*.

### You are the one

If you go into your thought, the creation is really '*me.*' I am the subject who creates 'I am.' Who's the judge who makes heaven and hell, ascending and descending? I am. I'm the one. When you realize this you become a really powerful person. You can go wherever you want—the horrible places, the beautiful places, the heavenly places—and everywhere you are blissful, every aspect is so beautiful. It's all in the

receiver, the one who is relating to it, the person who is receiving it—he who is 'I am.'

*you are important*
There is no one more important than yourself. It may seem very egotistic, but you are important. You can completely dominate yourself, make yourself a complete prisoner . . . or you can completely liberate yourself. We say that something makes me happy: a beautiful girl, a beautiful man, a beautiful home, lots of money, a rich country. But actually our thoughts create our world. If you carefully examine your thoughts, nothing else really makes you happy. None of these other conditions really affect you. You are the one who decides which way you want to take any situation or relationship: that's the way it works.

Meditation is live growth, or human potential. We can do just so much. We cannot physically change everything in the world, but our own energy, our being, this we can change. We have nothing more important than our 'beingness,' our own selves. As human beings, we can develop this through our own growth. You need to encourage yourself, because you have much great potential. We love to travel to

*a wider consciousness*
Europe, Asia, and different countries—or to the Moon, Mars, and different planets. But if you travel in this wider consciousness, there are many different realms. I'm not exaggerating: it seems there are different realms within consciousness. It's faster than flying in a plane. In a moment, a second, you can go into that consciousness. You can discover a different realm. Or at least you can find a different experience.

### Always within

Sometimes we may be concerned with death, or maybe with losing ourselves, or loneliness, or leaving this world. But all the scientists working together cannot go beyond space. We're always within. We always belong to the Buddha-field, or God-consciousness, or Infinite Mind. We are always united. There are many names: God, Jesus Christ, Buddha, or Enlightened. These statements have the same root. We look at history and interpret something finished in this world. And today we are here. If I truly speak, *they too are here*. If they are truly

*not separate*
enlightened, they are within everything—they have not gone anywhere. For example, Jesus Christ nailed to the cross is very symbolic: he is not separate. That is, Samsara and Nirvana, Illusion and Reality, are integrated, inseparable. And we too are already within that nature. We cannot be separated from that.

We are sometimes so lonely and sad—but we are not alone. Within our own awareness, there are many good friends. We can't separate ourselves from them. Still we have many fears . . . we are afraid, but we know this will change because these things are not permanent.

We can make friends with our own deeper realization: this is the best friend we can have. Whenever we have problems, we can ask and always get positive helpful answers. In the moment of suffering, we can always ask our own realization, and find encouragement, inspiration, and the path to enlightenment. We are lonely people—sometimes we are desperate. At these times, we must really encourage ourselves: our real family, our true home, is within. We can change difficult feelings into positive feelings of love.

*our own deeper realization*

We love entertainments and nice things. Once mind is transformed, any aspect—sound, form, friends ... every object in the world—becomes very beautiful. Everything shines. Everything becomes Beauty, or Art, or Music. Sometime you may be very surprised with *sound*. Even when you listen to your own sound, your own voice, there's something you can learn from it. Someone is internally communicating with you, and this experience can give you knowledge. Even looking at the leaves of a small plant can make something very clear to you. Every single aspect of existence becomes a kind of beauty. There's something you can learn from each experience. As your consciousness becomes transformed, natural insight develops.

Since we are always within that true nature, we can always rely on it completely. No matter what struggles or problems we have, we are still within the positive realm. When we understand that level of consciousness, we see we are in the very safest place. You may say we are in Samsara, but Samsara is within the Reality, the enlightened seed, and we are in that Seed.

*rely on it completely*

So if we look to our own true nature we can always see the positive side. We don't need to worry too much, or be too concerned. We have to face many difficulties, but all of them are a manifestation of our thoughts and concepts. At any time we can go into our thoughts, and the problems will dissolve, like a bubble.

### Bring the teachings alive

We have many ideas about the teachings, doctrines, interpretations, and sound. Our own voice is a teaching, our own sound is the doctrine, our own interpretation is the teaching. The teaching is introduced in order to finally realize something, but the teaching and the realization is not separate. Still, we have made mistakes, interpreted the doctrines or teachings wrongly, and categorized things so very strictly that we have drifted far from the Buddha's teachings. Today, because of so many unclear interpretations, we do not really understand the teachings. The teachings and our selves are not separate. But you say, 'not this, not that,' and divide everything. There is one beautiful divine nature, you say, but even that is cut up conceptually, negated

*the teaching*

logically, until there is almost nothing left. Then that divine nature is far away. What is negation? Our own concepts. Work with negative concepts for a long, long time, and finally you get nothing.

We have many problems, but if we can bring the teachings alive, awareness becomes fresh, alive within your own thought. This quality of aliveness is like light, so therefore we call it 'enlightened' or wisdom—no feelings of separateness, just completely free, completely positive, no problems, no negations. The characteristics of samsaric mind are no longer present. The mind becomes completely balanced. That's what meditation means, and this is what we need to practice.

*completely balanced*

Any moment, wherever you are, driving a car, sitting around, working, talking, any activities you have—even if you are very disturbed emotionally, very passionate, or even if your mind has become very strong, raging, overcome with the worst possible things and you cannot control yourself, or you feel depressed . . . if you really go into it, there's nothing there. Whatever comes up becomes your meditation. The more heated up you are, the more energy there is. Even if you become extremely tense, if you go into your thought and your awareness becomes alive, that moment can be more powerful than working for a long time on meditation practice. At those times, a very short moment can bring great results.

*awareness becomes alive*

There is nothing to throw away—even the most negative emotions are useful. The more you go into the disturbance—when you really get in there—the emotional characteristics no longer exist. Then this becomes proper meditation. Your experience becomes part of your realization. Maybe you can't find anything. If you are looking in a subject-object way, then you have problems. But if you really get into it, then there is nothing left—no anger, no greed, no lust. These are words which are terrible, negative, bitter—you don't even mention them. But even with these lower emotions, it's possible you can heat them up and stay in them. But don't lose the center. Go into the thought. When you're very heated up and you're in that nature, stay in the meditation. Soon the meditation has become very powerful. I think that is what they sometimes call the 'peak experience'—not the absolute experience, but a really good experience. Whenever you have distractions, go into it. Don't separate yourself from it. Don't separate yourself from your ego and that emotion. This way you become one, *into* one. Bring up as much fire, energy, as you can, and stay in it. Don't go away from it and don't separate yourself from it. You and your experience become united. Stay in it, be in it, and *still* it. Don't judge it. Just try to express it. If you can work with it, it may be very, very useful.

*peak experience*

We have a hard time facing things, always trying to escape, always running away from things. And we are tight . . . we hang on. We understand, in a way, what reality is, but on the other hand, we are

*K*hentse Rinpoche (mKhyen-brtse-chos-kyi-blo-gros), the Root Guru of Tarthang Rinpoche. He is the second Jam-dbyangs-mkhyen-rtse-dbang-po and an incarnation of Padma Sambhava. Khentse Rinpoche was the most excellent teacher during the first half of the twentieth century.

living today in Samsara, and we have to be concerned with morality. We have to be concerned with work, with society, with parents, with our reputation, our own name, and so on. We are tied up in every way. In a way, we are really prisoners here. Samsara is our prison . . . there is no freedom. Even in our own concepts, we don't think freely. If we think that way, we become guilty. "Oh, I shouldn't think about that." Immediately there is judgment. Our minds are so tight we can't even think freely.

*samsara is our prison*

These things happen in the human condition. But do the exercise--kind of secretly in a way--and get into the experience. You have to learn it. You cannot hide for a whole lifetime. You have to face it sometime. Facing it may be better than hiding, ignoring it, or trying to escape.

*meditation*

All these things start from thought. Thought is so simple. Whether past thought, present thought, future thought—anytime—try to exercise, go into the thought . . . and this becomes your meditation. What we're trying to do is not to make enemies of our thoughts—'you cannot contemplate, you cannot concentrate.' We need to break down that bridge of thought, and then become completely relaxed. Mind becomes still, and free, and that is our meditation. ❧

# The Life Story
# of Shakyamuni Buddha

*Although I showed you the means of liberation,*
*You must know that it depends on you alone.*

SHĀKYAMUNI

Ｔｗｏ ｔｈｏｕｓａｎｄ ｅｉｇｈｔ ｈｕｎｄｒｅｄ ｙｅａｒｓ ａｇｏ, the Bodhisattva, Mahasattva—who was to become the Tathagata Shakyamuni in his next birth—was preaching the Dharma to the Devas who inhabit the Tushita heaven. After absorbing himself in contemplation he looked out through the Three-thousand Great-thousand world systems and realized that it was time for him to take rebirth within the Jambudvidpa continent in the land of India.

## The Birth of Lord Buddha

In the city of Kaplivastu in Northern India, there reigned a great, noble Maharaja, named Suddhodana, or Pure Rice. His Kingdom was prosperous, his people were happy and without want, and the Maharaj was blessed with two fair and faithful wives, the two sisters Maya and Prajapati. But despite the wealth and peace of his Kingdom, the Maharaj was not satisfied, for he had no heir.

Then one night, the Maharini Maya dreamt that a great white elephant, with six tusks of the purest ivory, touched her on the right side with his trunk while she lay in a garden dressed in royal robes. When he touched her side, he seemed to melt and pass into her womb. When she awoke, the room was glowing with an orange light, and the music of unseen celestial musicians filled the air.

In the print [lower right], the Maharini is seen dreaming in her palace, and [top right] the great white elephant is seen attended by Devas.

Suddhodana rejoiced and called his seers who delivered the following interpretation and prophecy: "A Lord of men is to be born, but whether he will be a temporal or spiritual ruler is uncertain. If, when he is able to judge, he is to behold a sick man, an old man, a dead man, and a holy monk, then great and wide will be his kingdom, but not of this world. If he does not behold these things, he will be a Universal Ruler, great in riches, power and glory." Suddhodana, however, vowed that his son should never see these things, for he wished his son to become an even greater ruler than himself.

Soon the Maharini was heavy with child. After several months, the Maharini, accompanied by her sister Prajapati, traveled to the house of her parents—following the custom of her people that the child should be born there. During their journey, they passed the Lumbini Gardens in Southern Nepal, and Maya commanded the caravan to stop so that she might wander awhile in the cool shade of the trees.

In this garden, Maharini Maya felt the oncoming birth of the child. As she stood beneath a great palsa tree, she seized a bough of the tree, and the Bodhisattva emerged from her right side. His body and speech possessed the thirty-two marks and eighty characteristics of the perfected being, and when he emerged, it seemed to the handmaidens that the sun had just come from behind a cloud.

The new-born child took seven steps, and where he walked lotuses grew under his feet. Then he declared: "Thus have I come for the well-being of the world. This is my last birth!" The infant Prince, his right hand in the gesture of fearlessness, is shown before seven lotus blossoms [lower left], while above him Devas anoint his head with the nectar of immortality.

Suddhodana received his new-born son with greatest joy. But seven days later, the Maharini Maya, too full of joy, passed into the heaven realms. For this child was no ordinary mortal. In the print [upper left], two Devas are shown in Tushita heaven, holding the crown of the infant Prince who abandoned it to return to human incarnation. The new-born received the name, Siddhartha, "He who has attained his aim."

---

The first four woodblock prints belong to a design cut in Derge in Kham around 1720. They represent an influx of the Chinese Ch'ing style into Tibetan art with the arrival of the Ambans into Lhasa. Amban artists were successful in influencing Tibetan artistic life in the two big printing centers of Derge and Nar Tang.

The last print was drawn by Khamtrul Rinpoche at Trashi Jong in Kham, a monastery of the Drugpa sect, and the blocks were carved in Tubden Nam Gyal Gompa.

## The Prince Siddhartha

When the time came for Siddhartha's instruction, Suddhodana summoned the sage Vishvamitra. Yet when Vishvamitra questioned him, there was nothing Siddhartha did not know. In this scene [upper right], teacher and pupil are shown seated in a small pagoda.

Suddhodana was yet uneasy, and resolved that Siddhartha must never have the inclination or opportunity to renounce his kingdom. Thus Suddhodana built four palaces, one for each season, and took every care that Siddhartha should always be surrounded by sensual beauty. In the print, Siddhartha, attired in princely robes, is seated on a throne, with his father behind him, while lovely maidens sing and dance for his amusement.

Despite these many amusements and distractions, Siddhartha was not always happy. He would often withdraw from the many pleasures of the senses and spend hours in deep meditation. The Prince's periods of detachment greatly worried Suddhodana. So he sent for Yashodhara, the most beautiful princess of all the surrounding kingdoms. Yashodhara, a maiden of unblemished character, genuinely pleased the young Prince.

In accordance with custom, athletic contests were proclaimed to decide who should have Yashodhara's hand. Siddhartha, seemingly abandoning his previous detachment, joined the contests with a will. He showed himself superior in every way. First he is shown [lower right] with discharged bow, having just driven an arrow through the trunks of three trees and an iron pig's head. Above the archery scene, Siddhartha exhibits his skill in swimming, and [bottom left] is shown relaxing, having just tossed an elephant into a river.

Although Yashodhara proved to be a pleasant and faithful companion, Siddhartha still felt bound in his pleasure palaces and yearned to be free. One day, Suddhodana allowed his son to travel through the city by chariot, but only after strict instructions to the townspeople that the sick, old, or dead were not to be seen on Siddhartha's journey. But the Devas assumed human form to help fulfill the destiny of Prince Siddhartha. During the chariot ride, Siddhartha saw a sick man, an old man, and finally, the body of a dead man, over which two vultures were hovering. Thus were Siddhartha's eyes opened to the common lot of all incarnate life.

After meeting a holy man, shown with begging bowl and staff, Siddhartha resolved to renounce his inheritance and search for an escape from the chains of existence. One night, then, the attendants assigned to keep watch on the Prince unaccountably (again the work of Devas) fell asleep. Siddhartha, seeing his chance, saddled his faithful stallion and was accompanied by a host of Devas who held up the hooves of the animal lest they wake the sleeping Palace guards. The young prince thus left his father's Kingdom, in fulfillment of the prophecy which had attended his birth.

## The Great Renunciation

Far from his father's Kingdom, Siddhartha removed his jewels and ornaments, and, turning to his man-servant Khanda, said, "Take these jewels to my father and tell him that, with no lack of love or feeling of anger, I have entered the ascetic-wood to destroy old age and death." In the print, Siddhartha is shown in the act most symbolic of his great renunciation: with his knife he cuts off the knot of hair which as a Prince he wore twisted with jewels. Below him, attendant Devas catch the hair as it falls.

Then he traded his princely robes with a passing hunter who was attired in coarse red cloth. Above Siddhartha [to the left], are shown the Himalayan ascetics in their caves to whom Siddhartha went for teaching. Here, in the five-mountain Vindhya range, Siddhartha met the Brahman Alara who became his first teacher. Thus the young Monk learned the sacred scriptures and joined in the strong chanting of the Vedic hymns. When food was needed, he went to the city below, begging from house to house [bottom left].

But Siddhartha soon found that the singing of Vedic hymns and the learning of ancient scriptures did not satisfy his thirst for wisdom. Siddhartha then went to the renowned teachers Arada and Udraka, but was not satisfied, for they both clung to a concept of a soul, and in this the Bodhisattva perceived the seed of suffering. Thus exhausting the wisdom of the greatest teachers, Siddhartha resolved to go into the forest to practice the path of asceticism.

On the banks of the river Nirajnana, the Bodhisattva practiced the ascetic precepts. He practiced staring like a deer until he could gaze days without count into the horizon, forgetting the body and its pain, and forgetting the mind and its wandering. This he did for six long years, until his body withered to skin and bones. When he desired food, he would beg single grains of rice or single jujuge fruits, and in this way warded off death.

Yet Siddhartha discerned that he was still far from Nirvana. And so he abandoned the way of mortification and nursed his body back to health. On his way out of the forest, he received some milk and accepted an armful of pure and pliant Kusha grass from a farmer [lower right]. Then he made his way to Bodh Gaya. Spreading the grass beneath a Bodhi Tree, he seated himself with folded hands and feet, with the resolve to win complete enlightenment. Thus Siddhartha began his final fight with the many forms of Mara.

## The Final Enlightenment

The Bodhisattva Shakyamuni sat beneath the Bodhi Tree steadfast in his resolve to win perfect insight. Then Mara, the King of Desire, who brings delight to the senses and clouds the intellect, shot an arrow at the Lord and sent his daughters Lust, Delight, and Thirst with his sons Confusion, Gaiety, and Pride to disturb Siddhartha's calmness of mind.

Prithividevi [beneath Lord Buddha], appeared and knelt before him. Mara's daughters, appearing in the forms of beautiful young maidens, begged him to abandon his life of detachment and return to the ease and pleasures of his Kingdom. But through the power of the Bodhisattva, they became transformed into old women.

Then Mara, bitterly afraid and ashamed of defeat, ordered his army to attack the Bodhisattva with spears of copper, flaming swords, and cauldrons of boiling oil. They came riding decaying corpses, and lashing out with hooks and whips and spiked wheels of fire. Some sprouted flames from every hair, or rode mad elephants through the tree tops. The earth shook, and the regions of space flashed flames. Yet whenever any implement or barbed flaming destruction came near the Bodhisattva, it turned into a rain of flowers, fragrant and gentle to the touch. Then a voice from some celestial being addressed Mara saying, "O Mara, cease this vain fatigue. Throw aside enmity and retreat to peace. This sage will no more be shaken by you than Mt. Meru by a fickle wind." Mara, beaten, ceased his torment, and the Sage's mind was still.

Thus began the First Watch. As the east became grey, Shakyamuni, consciousness withdrawn into the Infinite, perceived a continuous vision of all his past lives and rebirths. In the Second Watch, our Lord beheld all that lives, and the transient round of birth and death of all mankind.

In the Third Watch, there came perception higher still, for he beheld the causes of the chain of existence and how all suffering proceeds from ignorance. Having thus perceived the world as it is, Shakyamuni was perfected in his wisdom. In him was completed the destruction of craving and desire, as a fire goes out for lack of fuel.

And so Siddhartha, "Accomplished of Aim," reached the final goal, for at that moment he became the Bhagavan, the Arhat, the Tathagata, the Sugata, the Anuttara Samyak Sambuddha—for he had obtained Perfect Enlightenment, Sambodhi.

With his right hand he touched the mat of grass beneath the Bodhi Tree and called all the Earth to witness his victory over Mara and his long-sought release from the round of birth and death. And the Earth shook in six ways.

## *Turning the Wheel of the Dharma*

After the Buddha attained complete enlightenment, he considered whether or not to preach the Dharma, for he thought no one would understand the depth of his experience. But Brahma, knowing the Sage's thought, left the Brahmaloka and appeared before the Buddha, saying, "Please do not pass into the forest like a rhinoceros and adopt the habit of a recluse. All the Sugatas of the past have fulfilled their vow and have turned the Wheel of the Immaculate Dharma. Do so likewise."

The Tathagata assented and thought that it would be best to preach to his five former ascetic companions. As Buddha approached Saranath, the five mendicants saw him coming, and said to one another, "There is Gautama who has abandoned the ascetic path for the luxuries of the world. Let us not rise to greet him, nor pay homage or offer him a seat." But when the Buddha approached, so powerful was his vow and so calm was his mind that against their wills they immediately rose and offered him the highest seat. One took his robe and one washed his feet while the others made respectful greetings. Then the Buddha said, "Do not address me by Gautama any longer, for I am the Buddha, and by my own effort I have attained the difficult to attain."

Thus he began turning the Wheel of the Dharma, teaching each according to their capabilities. For those of lesser understanding, he taught that Samsara is a burning house and that the discipline of a monk is the proper method to escape the Wheel of Birth and Death. For those of more advanced intellect, he taught that a compassionate intention towards all beings will liberate all of Samsara. And to those most advanced, he taught the method of recognizing non-dual insight and obtaining Buddhahood in a single lifetime.

In the print, the Tathagata is shown preaching the Lotus Sutra. When the Buddha was staying at Rajagriha, he illuminated the entire universe with a ray of light which sprang from his eyebrows. From the highest heavens to the lowest hell realms everything was illuminated by the ray. He especially illuminated those realms where other Buddhas were teaching the Lotus Sutra. He thus displayed this profound Dharma to monks and Bodhisattvas, to Devas and to men, whereby the miseries of all Samsara can be ended. ❖

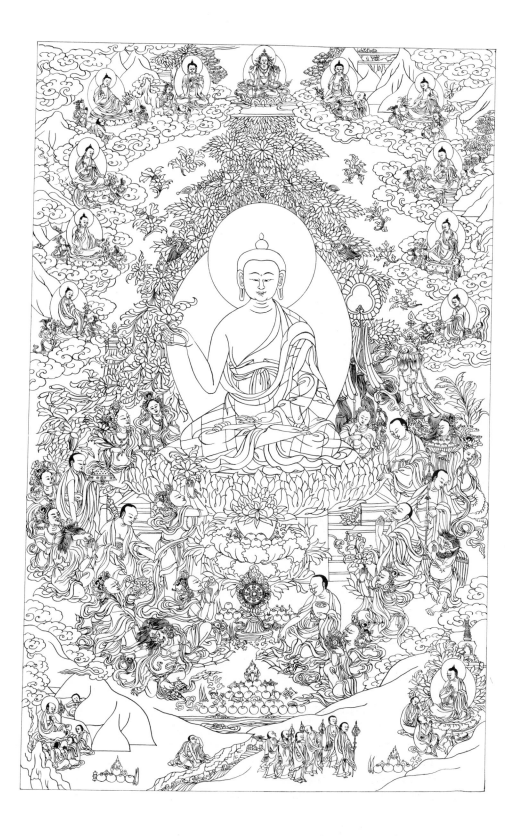

# The Self-Image

*A magic spell, a dream, a gleam before the eyes,*
*A reflection, lightning, an echo, a rainbow,*
*Moonlight upon water, cloud-land dimness*
*Before the eyes, fog and apparitions,*
*These are the twelve similes of the phenomenal.*

NĀROPA

THE NYINGMA TRADITION has many descriptions of what a human being is. Consciousness is pictured as a physical reaction. What a human being is inside is the same as what he or she is outside, in the physical realm. A human being *is* the embodiment of his consciousness. In other words, what it is to be a human being is the same physically as it is mentally. There is no difference. What a person thinks or feels—how he behaves on the physical level—reflects his present state of consciousness. A person's characteristic behavior patterns—his obsessions, his dullness, his unhappiness, or his feelings of great fulfillment—are all manifested on the physical level. We may say that a person is really functioning properly as a human being when his consciousness is well-balanced. If he has problems, such as mental or physical blockages, these difficulties can be seen on the physical level.

If we observe our constant play of thoughts and ideas, we will find that we have many thoughts and many conceptions about who or what we are. Our thoughts are so involved with a *self-image*! We expect ourselves to behave in certain ways. We see ourselves sitting in a certain way, or looking a certain way, or wearing certain kinds of clothes, or talking in a certain manner. All these are expressions of individual

*a*
*human*
*being*

characteristics which take on a separate form—a separate personality which is different from who we actually are.

### Recognizing the self-image

This self-image directly represents our level of consciousness. First, we create thoughts or thought-models which feed our consciousness. Then, our consciousness becomes involved in a different world, the world of our self-image. We could talk more philosophically about the various levels at which the self-image operates, but basically this is what the self-image is. Self-image is interesting because, when we examine it, it doesn't show itself. It cannot be pinpointed as anything. It disperses, it is nothing. True, you may have concepts about a certain self-image you may have at a particular time, but there is no *one* particular self-image that outlasts any conceptions you may have about it.

*self-image disperses*

We think and talk as if we could actually touch or see our self-image. What is important to understand is that there are actually two separate qualities acting: our self, or 'me' or 'I' . . . and our self-image. This 'me' or 'I' is involved with life in a multitude of ways. This 'I' experiences and feels and sees things in a way which is very alive, very immediate. But when this 'I' becomes imbued with the self-image, the person is not really himself—he is acting as if he were some other person. For example, you are tremendously shy, or you feel very shameful, embarrassed or guilty . . . or you feel afraid, your life is in danger, or you are dissatisfied. At this time the 'I' is overcome with a very vivid, very alive sensation which is really only the activation of the self-image. Two separate things are occurring. The first is the operation of the five *skandhas*, or 'elements,' which make up the human being. But apart from these there is an additional force which is the self-image.

*self, me, I . . . and self-image*

We can think, examine-meditate, and maybe make very clear to ourselves what kind of status we are giving to this self-image. Let us say you are watching your thoughts and emotions during some tremendous disturbance, some great sadness. Your mind is very agitated. At these times you might be able to observe that you are not actually the person who is experiencing this emotional state. You are actually not the person that is feeling great pain. You are not the one creating those disturbances. They are being created through the operation of your self-image. But sometimes this is hard to see because you are so involved with the self-image you have created throughout your life. What is essential for you to see is that, during those particularly painful disturbances, you have the opportunity to step back and actually see the core of your self-image. For instance, when certain energies develop—a trembling or volcanic sort of consciousness, or a feeling of fear, or anger, or tightness—what is creating this holding-strength is the self-image.

*holding-strength*

But just like the self-image, this holding-strength does not really exist. Just as there is no abiding 'self,' or 'ego,' there is also no abiding self-image. True, the actual feeling is there, but its holding-power will be completely lost as soon as you have lost your interest in feeding the self-image. At that time you can have a totally different experience than what you had thought was possible in that previous state of painfulness.

It is so easy to let the self-image perpetuate itself, dominate your whole life, and create an unbalanced state of affairs. You become a prisoner, or you feel you are inside a cage. You accept this blockage. In fact, some people don't really like to act in different ways, even if the present situation invites a new response. Such a person almost always moves in predictable ways. On the physical level, he has difficulties. He may feel a tightness, a restrictiveness. He doesn't want to open up to other people's gestures or expressions. He could act in different ways, he could initiate different gestures, but he is like a sick man. The self-image is like a disease that is attached to the person: it is fixed to him and he acts in a restricted way.

So, how can we involve ourselves less with our self-image, and how can we make ourselves more flexible? We are human beings, not animals, and we do not have to live as if we were in cages or in bondage. At the present level, before we start meditating on the self-image, we do not realize the difference between our self-image and our 'self.' We do not have an access-gate or point of departure. But if we can recognize just some small difference between our self-image and our self, or 'I' or 'me,' we can then see which part is the self-image. Once we have recognized the self-image, we will see that it has characteristics which are not flexible, not lucid. It is like a yak's horn, hard, restricted and narrow. The self-image does not allow anything to enter other than its own rigid constructions. It does not accept. But unless we actually see the self-image for what it is, it is difficult for us to willingly admit that these sorts of things are actually happening to us.

### Looking

In order to make ourselves more flexible, we must first learn to recognize this self-image. *It is not you.* All this is a very big subject, but here we are talking about self-image in a simple, practical way. For example, we are experiencing an emotional disturbance. Maybe we have feelings of very deep physical dissatisfaction. When you imagine or think about it, the thoughts and feelings are almost visible. Perhaps it is a sexual problem. Many people feel frustrated. They feel energy blockages. This may be due to a great deal of fantasizing which creates an image, an idea, which can never be experienced in reality. At the same time, a person may feel tremendous energy. But his energy is frustration-energy. He feels as if his energy is being drawn away—self-drowning, completely hopeless, a feeling of desperation. His emotions feel very thick, dense, dark and confused—there is no light. This energy of frustration causes the person to want to cry, but he does not know why. He hasn't any reasons or explanations for this unhappy state. Energy is drawn up, then it collapses completely. The person feels drowned in his own sorrow. There is no life, no light, no positive feelings. At this time, he has many fantasies, dreams and expectations—but none of these things happen. Nothing comes alive. All that he experiences is the expression of what he would *like* to have happen. These kinds of feelings cause him to remain in his own realm, his own world. His self-image is keeping him there. But if he lets go of that energy, that holding-power, he can immediately separate himself from it: instantly he feels different. Something very different definitely happens, but a person may not exactly understand what it is unless he has this experience.

You can especially learn this awareness, or 'looking,' when you have obsessions or fantasies. You can see the restrictive self-image and separate yourself from it. Suppose you do not have any good friends and you feel very lonely. You want to be happy. You want to make your fantasy more vivid, more alive. You can almost see it, feel it, touch it. For instance, men, in their heads, do a lot of fantasizing about women's bodies, and the opposite is true for women. In this imagining, a person creates sensational feelings and generates much energy. You can feel that energy and vividly visualize it. Use this fresh energy to arouse your awareness to separate you from your self-image-making—and immediately look back at your situation.

*arouse awareness*

To recognize this energy before it consumes you, you must develop an awareness that can look back at the situation you have created. At this time the energy-strength is felt very differently—it is like two different worlds, two different kinds of energies. But when you step back, then you can use this fresh energy to see the world of your involvement with the self-image.

*energy-strength*

### Feeding the self-image

What we created initially was the self-image—we are perpetuating something we can never satisfy. We will never find any satisfaction because we are not feeding the right person, which is our real self. Instead, this nourishment goes to our self-image.

When we eat, we do not know exactly where the food goes. We know that it has combined with different substances in our body and has actually become a different substance—the original substance no longer

exists. In the same way, our thoughts and emotions are conceptually feeding our self-image.

There is a simple children's illustration which is useful. In Tibet, there are many groundhogs. In the wintertime, the bears like to eat the groundhogs who hibernate underground. So the bear digs around, finds a groundhog, hits it, and, thinking he has killed it, sets it aside for later. But the groundhog wakes up and runs away. Again, the bear digs around and finds another groundhog, hits it hard, and sets it aside. Then he wants to find *more*. But meanwhile, all the groundhogs run away and he has nothing left but the one he is holding.

In this way, we keep feeding our desires without ever being satisfied. We can never feel fulfillment or satisfaction because every-thing is going to feed our self-image. We deny our self the real satis-faction and give it to the wrong person. It is true that sometimes we have a chance to find satisfaction in our feelings, in our physical or mental needs. At those times, it is really *you yourself* that finds fulfill-ment—you feel open and clear and balanced. But most of the time we are working for the self-image and feel constricted. *feeding desires*

The self-image is not connected to anything—it is nothing but our imagination. But sometimes certain forms of our self-image can create definite sensations. Often it is very difficult for us to determine whether certain sensations arise from us or from our self-image. Let us say our sensations create enjoyable feelings of importance or goodness or security. But the self-image has a very grasping nature. Holding on to the enjoyment and trying to make sensations permanent develops feelings of tightness. This self-grasping is always making demands and causing us, finally, to be dissatisfied with our present experience. We can never *have* enough. *self-grasping*

Many of us have very creative minds and are able to visualize and fantasize very well. As a consequence, our self-image gets fed very regularly. For example, you would like to have the experience you are creating in your mind but you cannot have it because the energy you are creating is going to the self-image. You have certain physical needs and you want certain sensations fulfilled. But you feel deep dissatisfac-tion, as if there is a crying or a deep hurt within your subconsciousness. It is a very cloudy feeling, not happy or clear . . . a sort of moodiness inside that is like the atmosphere just before it rains. So, how do we work with the self-image? First, recognize the self-image, and secondly, jump away from it and look at it—because the self-image is not *you*.

### Skillful change

Many people go through life without ever changing certain facial expressions, gestures, or bodily postures. The way they choose to live is always the same—it never changes. They are completely permeated by the self-image. We need to see this rigidity in ourselves and work to change ourselves. For example, every time you think you are not happy say, "*I am happy.*" Say it strongly to yourself, even if your feelings are contradictory. Remember, it is your self-image, not you.

Maybe it is very logically true that you have difficulties. Say you don't have any money, or any friends, or a nice house, or a job. Maybe you are not liked by others, or you are not beautiful. We can find all sorts of rational excuses for our difficulties. But you must forget the rational side. You must understand that you are not happy because your feelings are very clouded. You feel uncertain. It is a dark, heavy feeling that dominates your whole being. You are not open. But just as fast as a fish can move in the water, you can instantly change to a happy attitude, a balanced attitude. Keep yourself there. Believe yourself. Be open to that positiveness. Your whole inner situation can change, even if the external conditions do not change right away. If you want to feel positive and have satisfaction, then be open and flexible. *You have the choice.*

It is true that at certain times you are not happy. Certain things are occurring in a way you do not like. Immediately, at such a time, mentally change your concept. All you need to do is take a different perspective. When you do this, you will see the self-image creating disturbances. When you look back at the self-image, you don't want to believe you are that person. You don't really want to look. You are afraid you will see that your consciousness is dependent on so many conditions. So you need to understand that consciousness is really quite flexible.

Our consciousness does not have a diamond-like quality in its present form. It is not yet indestructible. So it is important to develop flexibility in our consciousness. We can practice changing from unhappiness: completely believe the unhappiness in your mind and feelings, and then change it . . . like a fish which can quickly change direction in the water. Its body has almost an electric swiftness and sharpness. This energy is very subtle. So in the beginning, try to develop this skill of *changingness.* This skill develops acceptance, not in the heavy way—"I need to accept this"—but in a simple way, just feeling the experience happening. In this way you give yourself the choice to develop very effective or skillful changes whenever you are confronted with negative experiences. First, *be* the experience, completely accept it. Then jump to the positive side. How is it? You can clearly see the differences between the positive and negative experiences. Then you can almost experience both at the same time. Jump from one side to the other and then back again. You will see there is no 'from,' there is only awareness.

*instantly change*

*consciousness is flexible*

*first be the experience*

This experience is something like looking into a mirror. From this awareness you can see where you are now and how it was before. You can almost simultaneously feel two different atmospheres. Then you can make the choice to develop the self-image side which makes you a prisoner. Or, you can stay with the positive side which is a feeling of lightness, fullness, and wholeness. No desiring, no unfulfillment. You yourself are balanced, and everything is interesting for you just as it is. You become no more or no less than what you are. You feel no impediments, no distractions, no obstacles. Your feelings and your mind no longer feel so divided. You do not feel agitated or restless. You do not feel you have to go somewhere, because you are feeding yourself directly, instantly. There is no dominating, conceptual self-

*you*
*yourself*
*are*
*balanced*

image taking you away from the immediacy of your being. You feel complete just as you are. But when you are dominated by your self-image, you are not independent, you are not liberated. You feel pressured, under the control of some unidentifiable agent. You have chosen to allow yourself no choice. This is what the self-image perpetuates. As long as you are involved with your self-image, you have no real feeling of completeness, no kingdom. Once your consciousness is thinking in terms of the self-image, you are no longer free.

We must learn to deal with this self-image by first of all recognizing it for what it is and then acting differently. Our concepts and feelings create our consciousness, whether we are happy, sad, or not affected. To do this, we must accept certain ways or attitudes that may be different from ones we are familiar with. We need to learn to act differently. This is possible because there is nothing in us that is substantial. The 'actor' is not solid. Even so, we feel we do not want to change. We may be unwilling to see situations differently. This is the strength of our self-image. We don't seem to want to give up this bondage, this samsaric suffering, because we feel we have to maintain our position as servant to our self-image. In other words, we are addicted to suffering. We seem to love suffering. We seem to need suffering. We almost have to be in some kind of suffering in order to live out our life. These are all characteristics of our self-image. Even if we consciously say to ourselves that we do not want to suffer and we do not want to go through this—we still must go through these experiences. We must live them out. This is the difficult part.

Because the self-image does not really exist, it is very difficult to deal with. You cannot exactly catch it. But at the same time it dominates us and controls us and makes us miserable. We can say we don't want to be miserable. But unless we come to some conclusions about what makes us suffer, we are only playing a game with ourselves. We cannot gain anything spiritually, or intellectually, unless we come to certain conclusions about the cause of our suffering. Otherwise we cannot become enlightened. We will not be able to achieve anything positive unless we choose for ourselves an attitude that is balanced, happy, and satisfied. No matter what situation we find ourselves in, we have the choice of which way we would like to go. Mentally healthy, a balanced mind, feelings of satisfaction . . . these are all humanly very acceptable. If we can succeed in these things—which is like looking for knowledge or wisdom—our whole life will have purpose. Otherwise, we are just very casually playing in Samsara. If we want a healthy attitude, then we can decide. ✤

# A Look into the Sky-like Mirror

*A look into the sky-like mirror*
*which is Mind as such*
*by which the nature of the Absolute,*
*in which neither bondage nor freedom exist,*
*is elucidated.*

*I bow to the gentle splendor of Samantabhadra,*
*the self-existing impulse of all life.*

THIS IMPULSE [*rig-pa*] *which has nothing about it*
*so that it could be found as this or that*
*Is the self-existing pristine cognition with no*
*periphery or center.*
*When it is seen in the course of the Guru's instruction*
*It is the real spontaneous pristine cognition*
*to which everything points.*

This is the real presence of Reality to which everything points;
This presence has nothing of an intellectual creation about it.
This is the absolutely real in all reals,
Beyond cause and condition, it never changes or steps out of itself
      throughout time.

In this Absolute-as-genuineness, that cannot be pointed out
      by the mind,
All the varied reals are perfect in self-sameness.
The manifestation of its inherent creative motive force
      is the appearance of mind with its eight structural patterns.
It is in this mind that the multiple manifestations
      of Samsara and Nirvana occur.

The extent of this occurrence is a free occurrence
      in and as the ground as pure fact,
And as pure fact it is unconcerned with profit or harm,
      acceptance or rejection.
In not knowing the presence of pure fact, but
By being taken in by its creative motive force as an ontological
      principle, the notions of subject and object
      become even more hardened.

It is in their range that the variety of happiness and sorrow,
      profit and harm is experienced;
Appearing as such a variety, there is nothing in it as such.
It is the power of these fictions of one's own mind
      that is of benefit or harm.

Since beginningless time until now
Whatever there has been experienced of happiness and sorrow
      here in Samsara
Has never been something as such, but are the empty tricks of one's mind.
The unceasing manifestation is nothing else but jugglery.

Since the mere fact of mind, indivisibly luminous and open,
Is not sullied by any defects or virtues as represented by
      Samsara or Nirvana,
Even if one experiences the torments of the lowest hell,
Mind is not in the least hurt by them.

Whatever pleasures of and in the world may be felt,
They do not change the Absolute in any way.

The defects and virtues experienced as happiness and sorrow
Do not cling to it, as little as does dye to the sky.

Just as when a crystal is changed by a color and
One at that occasion clings to its appearance as
        this or that color,
So the various displays of the power of the fictions of the mind
As well as the various arguments in the countless
        philosophical systems,
Are set up by the mind, and all the ideas of the intellect
Are not what they seem to be;
They fade away in the Absolute which is not found
        as a concrete reality.

If one knows what is meant by the Absolute, uncreated, non-subjective,
It is by knowing one's reality that all reality is free in itself.
The jungle of philosophical systems with their postulates of finality
        comes to rest in themselves,
And the whole of the phenomenal world is present
        as Dharmakaya's realm.

Free from all beginning, free as such, free in its presence,
        free in its self-sameness,
Beyond the postulation of negation and affirmation, of acceptance
        and rejection, and
The expanding center in which all the entities of Samsara and Nirvana
        are complete in their self-sameness
By being of the nature of pure fact, actuality, and responsiveness—
The one and only creative point, the meaning of self-existent
        pristine cognition—
Its understanding is said to be the 'Great Perfection.'
This is the goal, the one pursuit, the climax of all pursuits.
Compared with this, all other pursuits with their acceptance
        and rejections, affirmations and negations,
Are called a pursuit of a path that is intellectually contrived.
They are all steps to this pursuit.

The stages on the path as outlined by specific philosophical systems
As well as all the arrangements of the spiritual levels and paths,
When they have been ascertained as the absolute certainty
        of Buddha awareness,
Come to their end effortlessly in the self sameness of Reality.

*He who runs after the fictions of his own mind*
*Is fettered or freed by the power of these fictions,*
*But he who knows the Absolute that is without fiction*
    *and the same forever,*
*Is one in whom from the beginning neither bondage nor freedom*
    *is observed.*

*While one will never be satisfied with however many pleasures*
    *one may have*
*In this Samsara—a self-deception*
*By one's own mind, like the appearances of a dream—*
*One will also never be weary even if one experiences*
    *hundreds of woes.*

*Fettered by one's own mind that appears*
*As this or that without limits, one roams about incessantly;*
*But when one understands the meaning of the Absolute*
    *where there is neither bondage nor liberation,*
*One has found the unchanging great bliss.* ❖

MI-PHAM 'JAM-DBYANG RNAM-RGYAL RGYA-MTSO

PART TWO

# PSYCHOLOGY

# Transmuting Energies
# through Breath

*There is tranquility and insight*
*In relying on the real foundation of life*
*Because of fusing mind with mind*
*And discriminating the whole of reality.*

MAHĀYĀNA-SŪTRĀLAṄKĀRA

WE CAN TRANSMUTE negative feelings into positive, balanced feelings. This does not mean just trying to be happy, because happiness is not necessarily balanced. Negativity is often based on frustration. But if mind and breath are functioning properly, negativity will not arise. It is very important to become conscious of our own breath. *We must not waste our breath*: breathe quietly and use your breath as little as possible.

*don't*
*waste*
*breath*

When breath is not balanced, many thoughts and concepts arise. Our breath is like an expansive lake with very still water. This lake reflects the things around it very beautifully. If we disturb this lake by, say, throwing a rock into it, the lake can no longer reflect the things around it beautifully. An image is no longer formed. So, we can discover what disturbs us by watching our breath.

There are actually two types of breath. The first is the outer breath, which is our normal breathing pattern. When a person begins to really meditate, this outer breath almost disappears. At the same time, this person does not have any feeling of tenseness as if his breath has been taken away. It is felt more as a loss of roughness of his outer breath. Yet, there emerges an inner breath that is soft and calm—a very relaxed form which is not something you need to think about. It is very enjoyable, comfortable, and full of feeling. This breath has the quality of quietness. It has a very relaxing, soothing quality.

There is very important energy in this breath. We must learn to develop this breath in order to become balanced. But this inner breath is so easy to lose. In order to learn how to keep this breath, we must first learn in what ways we are spending this breath. We can observe that we mostly spend our breath verbalizing. As we talk, each word we use is going to our thoughts. And our breath, like a horse, tires as it runs. If we carefully watch our vocalizations, we can see how our energy level is drained. So use as little energy as possible verbalizing.

There are two types of speculations that spend our energy. The first is image-like speculation: image after image, we are living in our mind, in a completely different world. The other type of speculation is verbal, such as talking or conversing. Often it is necessary to express ourselves to others in relationship as communication. But otherwise we must use as little breath as possible in verbal speculation, so that our energy does not collapse into depression. For example, yesterday something particular happened, today we find we need to repeat it verbally, and tomorrow we will need to explain things that happened today, and so on. This kind of circulation of speculation continues our whole lives.

Verbal speculation causes us much unhappiness, as well as wasted energy. In listening to ourselves or others, we agree or disagree . . . then opinions form and arguments or negativity may be created. But the less we breathe, the more calm we become. It is this calm, inner breath which we can transmute into blissfulness. The more we relax into this breath, the more we will find that this breath is energy. This energy has great value or potential. There can be much meaning within this breath. It can produce tremendous positive feelings. With concentration, this soft breath can flow to all parts of the body.

The body has within it various emotional centers or *chakras*. If we channel these energies properly throughout these centers, certain reactions are automatically produced. So we need to transmute these energies in a positive way through the breath.

As this breath circulates itself throughout all the emotional centers in the body, all kinds of blockages can be removed. In less than one second this breath can circulate all through the body to all the emotional centers. The inner-breath moves that fast.

We need to learn to develop this breath so that it can make us tranquil. It can completely relieve us of all our tensions or blockages. With these negative emotions we become so blocked, so rigid . . . we don't want to move, we don't want to open, we don't want to accept. We are thinking in an absolutely rigid way . . . we don't want to think in any other way. Finally, we despair—we may even try suicide because we think there are no solutions to our problems. If we thought there was a solution, we would not give up. These situations arise because we have not learned to control our breath from the beginning. Before anything happens, we must learn to always keep the breath very calm, very soft . . . little movement, not too much action. This is a very soothing and pleasant feeling, producing warmth in various degrees. As we continue to practice this breathing concentration or exercise, our bodies can become completely relaxed. This is a unique way to transmute blockages into very blissful, very sensitive feelings. The feeling and the breath become like a marriage. This positive feeling, this blissful feeling, this enjoyable, inexpressible feeling . . . all this is contained in this soft, inner breath. So, bring the feelings and breath into union. In time, all this will come. ❖

*transmuting blockages*

# Western Psychology
# Meets Tibetan Buddhism

*Watch without watching for something. Look*
*From the invisible at what you cannot grasp*
*As an entity. To see and yet to see no things*
*Is freedom in and through yourself.*

TILOPA

Anyone who arrived at 1815 Highland Place two days before the official opening of the Nyingma Institute would have seen roofers, painters, carpenters and upholsterers busy at work, and debris piled high in the parking lot—in short, a catastrophe. The Padma Ling students, with a few volunteers, had worked around the clock. On June 24th, the arriving 'students' found clean if spartan quarters, and were a little surprised to be handed brooms and mops. This was not the smoothly staffed American institution they were used to; instead, they were expected to help keep the place clean, clear the garden of broken glass, and help prepare or clean up after meals. Our very arrival was an immediate lesson in the Buddhist secret of survival, a philosophy which

---

GAY GAER LUCE wrote the following article after attending the Human Development Training Program, an eight-week intensive seminar offered at the Nyingma Institute for professionals in the helping professions. A writer and psychologist, she is the author of *Body Time*, works as a therapist, and teaches *sKum Nye* at the Nyingma Institute.

urges the acceptance of life as it is, rather than an effort to meet expectations. The Institute was the opposite of all that is institutional: nobody could be a passive recipient of food, lodging and instruction without becoming part of a community. Similarly, the instruction was often socratic, involving direct experience and very little book work.

*summer training program*

During the summer training program, we spent seven or eight hours together in class, with assigned practices that should have absorbed another four hours—a full day. From 8 A.M. to 5 P.M. we sat on folded pillows in an incense-fragrant room, the lama seated before us on a raised platform, relaxed, and informally talking in a manner that was deceptively simple. He asked a few questions. "What is the difference between calmness and stillness? . . . What is sound?" We gave the articulate answers one might expect of educated professionals: "Sound is the pressure of air waves on the eardrum, a physiological response, a pattern of neuronal activity, etc." But as we listened to ourselves we began to get the message: what we accept for answers is simply the reduction of one concept or construct to another. We knew little about the experience of sound—although we were sitting in a relatively noisy room, over a street with some traffic. Noise, as Rinpoche observed, is a problem in America which can be destructive and create tension and disturbed thoughts. But there are many ways to experience sound. For instance, we were asked to become the sound, putting our entire consciousness into it. Then he asked us to see with our ears, listen with our eyes. This exercise was calculated to make one realize how much conscious control we can exert over sensory functions that seem fixed and involuntary. Actually one can alter the habit of hearing so that sounds produce images of bodily sensations.

*experience sound*

That first week it was difficult to sit still and watch our experience. We were discovering how heavily we had come to rely on words and constructs, experiencing the world in terms of discriminations and differences. Western education fosters a dualistic mode of thinking, and we tend to focus first on what is external to ourselves, learning to drive a car before we have learned to control our minds. To sit quietly for five minutes without entertaining a thought or image is not so easy.

We may have imagined we were relaxed, but we had yet to learn physical and mental relaxation before we could start to concentrate. "Deep relaxation can alter all of living," Rinpoche said. "When you are tight you cannot feel. Go deep. There is calmness and understanding there . . . satisfaction. Others cannot always please us, but in meditation we can learn to please ourselves." To relax, he taught us uniquely Tibetan forms of self-massage of the face, neck and upper body, using strong pressures, verging on painful. Many of the relaxation exercises were familiar: breathing in unison, listening to one's heartbeat, or

*deep relaxation*

chanting. Ironically, instead of bliss, some of us were now aware of muscle tensions we hadn't noticed before, inhibited feelings that crept out in tears, and the unruly noisiness of our minds, which kept up a kind of ceaseless chatter whenever we tried to be still.

Rinpoche offered special practices for physical relaxation and concentration to help us diminish the conversation in our heads. Sometimes we visualized complex images in dynamic interaction. Vajrayana Buddhism relies heavily upon visualization, a method that is *visualization* alien to most of our academic training. Generally it is assumed that eidetic imagery vanishes when children reach about age eight, yet Rinpoche can glance at a painting, and later close his eyes and see it in detail. Many artists cannot do this. As a Stanford University design professor has complained, many engineering and architecture students cannot visualize. "They can talk about it, not see it or draw it." Perhaps because we rely so heavily on language, we cultivate the functions of our left hemisphere at the neglect of the right. Thinking themselves "non-visual," many people accept this label as a physiological axiom rather than a habit. Our culture fosters a kind of snobbish self-approval in the articulate person, despite the fact that language is linear and inadequate to express complicated concepts. Einstein and other creative scientists have often mentioned the need to think in images.

Visualizing, like learning tennis, merely takes practice and energy. However, it was easier for me to follow a tennis teacher who in- *practice* sisted I practice a serve, than to be told I must spend six hours gazing *and* at a white Tibetan letter on a black background. I remember worrying *energy* that it would be six long hours of fruitless boredom. Physical action and small rewards keep one going in a sport, but in practicing mental functions, many many hours of inaction may pass before there is the incredible joy of really seeing that image, three-dimensional and bright, hanging in the blackness. One should be able to see any image, at will, and hold it for long periods of time without interference from thoughts or sense perceptions. This is just a first step in learning to meditate, and it seemed an impossibility to many of us.

Unused to sitting cross-legged on the floor, quite a few people found themselves distracted by painful ankles, lower back aches, unwanted itches, and extremities tingling with poor circulation. A few people gave up the posture and sat in chairs or leaned against walls and pillars. Rinpoche seemed to sense our discomfort and usually followed a period of physical stillness with stretching exercises that he usually initiated without announcement by making the movements himself.

Never having taught large groups in a Western manner, Rinpoche was sometimes hard to see and follow, for he did not always repeat himself or explain. Suddenly, during a tea break he would have the entire group picking glass fragments out of the parched earth

behind the house. This abruptness, characteristic of religious schools in the Near and Far East, keeps students on the alert. A Chilean-born psychiatrist and teacher who has written extensively on the progression from psychotherapy to spiritual quest (*The One Quest*), Claudio Naranjo studied Rinpoche's teaching style with deep interest. "He always talked at different levels. I would think he was talking directly to my needs, but he made everyone in the room feel that he was the center. . . ."

*different levels*

Most of the participants had taught, or lectured to large audiences, but Rinpoche had a way of putting us on the spot so that our pose of confidence was stripped away. He would pick out someone hiding in the back and ask a direct question. Or he created games. "Describe meditation in three words," he demanded. "But no word repeated." If the fortieth person repeated, Rinpoche remembered and jumped on him with glee. "Tranquility is used!" Without warning he would begin a new topic, beckoning a volunteer to come and stand before him, and then begin kneading his sternum with a thumb.

*physical exercises*

A kind of therapy similar to that developed by Wilhelm Reich is just now beginning to come into use. Vigorous and demanding physical exercises for cathartic effect or to awaken new states of mind have been well-known to the Tibetans for close to 1,400 years. One of the newer therapies, bioenergetics, consists of exercises developed by one of Reich's students, Alexander Lowen. These are, like many Tibetan practices, vocal and sometimes painful. Roughly speaking, they are designed to release blocked emotional energies that have been frozen into lifelong body postures, as anxiety is sometimes held in a tightly indrawn stomach. One similar exercise we used during the summer—the Vajra Asana—required us to stand in a very difficult position for five to ten minutes.

Within twenty seconds, knee and thigh pain began. Soon the body started to tremble. As the pain grew stronger, it was tempting to rest, but Rinpoche was omnipresent, stop-watch in hand, glaring at whoever was ready to give up. In a minute and a half the pain seemed unendurable, and in reaction many of us found ourselves angry, frustrated, almost sobbing with self pity. Five minutes seems an eternity the first time. After two minutes we began chanting "Om"—a choral groan of agony. Yet, somehow the unendurable became bearable. When the time was up, we lay down for 30 minutes panting in relief. "Control your breathing," we were told. Soon, as in a cold shower after a sauna, we went from a deep catharsis into peace and then into an experience of being energized from every cell.

In bioenergetics, and other Western therapies, stressors are used to unblock emotional energy, but Tibetans go a step beyond catharsis. All emotions, positive or negative, are considered forms of a basic energy. A stress position is merely a way of evoking frustration and pain, to be transformed into pure energy and then used in intensifying a visualization, or to lift a person out of a depressed or hostile mood. *basic energy*

One Texas school teacher in our midst would do such exercises for a half hour as a stimulant when he felt sluggish, but few others did it on their own. We are lazy, as Rinpoche remarked. Moreover, most of us have learned to dread pain, and we create even more distress in our avoidance. It is possible to concentrate on pain unemotionally, with detachment. At that point it turns into pure sensation, a form of energy, a plausible method for enhancing mental vitality.

These Tibetan exercises cannot be considered as medical or psychiatric devices apart from the philosophy in which they evolved. They were not intended to be simply means of handling particular situations. They are integrated into a whole view of life—one that has little sentimentality about death, pain, dirt, or human nastiness. These are not avoided, but seen and accepted. Enlightenment is said to be the ability to live with reality as it is, which means that one must peel away the culture's veneer over the nature of survival or life's brevity. Tibetan prayer beads, used as a kind of rosary, often contain a bead of human bone to remind the adept that all things, including himself, are transient. *a whole view*

This philosophy requires strength and self-mastery, which have never been considered explicit aims of Western schools, nor the antidote for emotional and psychosomatic illness. Buddhist therapy assumes that the person to be helped must have or acquire an unembellished view of reality, and that self-transcendence is the path toward health. Although some of the new therapies (Psychosynthesis, Transpersonal therapy, Biofeedback, etc.) take this view, Western medicine is predominantly oriented around treating problems, such as a symptom, drug abuse, depression, phobias. "What I mainly learned here," remarked Mark Baras, "was how limited my concept of therapy has been. Ninety percent of what we are concerned with would be a joke to Rinpoche." The Western therapist would try to help his patient with the so-called presenting problem, were it a migraine headache, fear of darkness, or a poor marriage. The symptom might be seen as the first of a string of problems that could be traced back to childhood. A Buddhist might see no problem at all, except in the person's current expectations and attitudes. Americans, particularly, feel that life is abnormal when it is not happy and smooth, but Buddhists accept that suffering is part of the human condition. Rinpoche convinced at least a few of the participants that Western psychotherapy and particularly analysis may create more problems than it solves. Many children, and adults, blame their parents for defects that Tibetans assume to be the inevitable flaws of the human condition. Psychotherapies often encourage this retrospective anger by magnifying past deprivations and focussing upon defects in parent-child relationships.

Like most Asians, Tibetans revere their elders and maintain family harmony even at some cost to the individuals. From Rinpoche's eyes we Americans are restlessly mobile. We express so much dissatisfaction with our country, that we seem to be unaware—as he sees it—that we live in a golden age of affluence and religious freedom. Appreciate it and enjoy this rarity in earth's history, he kept saying. But our family life puzzled him. There seemed to be so much disharmony, and the nuclear family without room for the aged seemed cruel. One of the most compelling themes of the entire summer was compassion. Sensing that we were frequently cut off from feeling, or that we tended to hide behind professionalism, Rinpoche gave exercises such as asking us to recall our earliest childhood and the way our parents nurtured us—feeding, bathing and nursing us at the helpless stage of infancy. How could we possibly repay them for giving us life? Instead of blaming parents for present dissatisfactions, he urged, we should try to visualize their sufferings, their impoverished or neglected lives, and especially feel the loneliness of old people, so fragile and overlooked.

Although nobody could be untouched by Rinpoche's own depth of compassion, many of the psychotherapists insisted that they had to deal with their patients' problems in Western terms. By the end of the summer, a few had changed. Aubrey Lindgren, who learned

*Buddhist and Western therapy*

*reverence for elders*

Gestalt from the late Fritz Perls, said, "I've been a problem-oriented therapist for the last 8 years, with drug addicts and people who are considered the victims of the world. Now I don't see myself working with their problems—I would rather help them appreciate the remarkable fact of being alive, and have a more serene existence regardless of their circumstances." Every few days, Rinpoche, with a mischievous gleam, would bait us to demonstrate how we, the professional experts, went about helping people. "I have a problem," he would announce, grinning broadly. "I don't believe in myself—how would you help me?" It was a losing game to answer professionally. We were not ready to ask what lies behind self-belief; indeed, what is the concept of self? Insofar as the lama could see, the theories underlying our professionalism were hopelessly fragmentary and confused, like Freud's Oedipal theory.

*professional problem-solving*

It was inevitable that we should come to a hilarious confrontation over Freud, and American sexual hangups that were unheard of in Tibet. "Why do you not relax?" he would ask, regarding sex. "When you have big expectations, you cannot feel." Our high expectations caused tensions that prevented pure sexual experience and enjoyment —and pseudo-medical manifestos demanding orgasm were at fault with the rest of the culture. Our culture overloads sex with so many associations—prestige, money, emotional needs (dependency, ascendency, etc.), along with irrelevancies built up by ads, TV, and movies—that few people have plain unalloyed sexual experience. As we tried to reach an understanding about basic sexuality in discussing Freudian theory, Rinpoche commented that Freud, a product of Western sexual confusion, could never have intended to say that children were *sexually* attracted to their parents. Therapists in the group wagged their heads, referred to cases, and heartily disagreed. But Rinpoche was emphatic. "Impossible!" he said. He was so emphatic that it prompted one young man to assert that he was attracted not only to his mother, but his father as well. Rinpoche was totally dumbfounded. "To your parents?" he asked, incredulous. When the laughter died down, it was clear that he referred to a basic physical drive, and purely physical attraction. To us, sexual attraction meant those many nuances and associations that might lead to sexual thoughts or intercourse. He meant sex. We were talking about S*e*x.

*sex*

We were not yet capable of teasing apart the many elements of our experience, to see what aspects were based on concepts, conditioned emotions, or accidental associations. It was not until much later that our mental exercises began to give us the tools we needed to analyze our own experience. We may have been professionals at verbal analysis, but in the land of interior feeling, we were fumbling.

*mental exercises*

At the bottom of a great deal of violence and sickness is the inability to handle emotions. In extremes, for instance, it shows up in the fact that over 60,000 U.S. children are brutalized every year, usually by parents who have no idea that there is any way of controlling the emotions they feel. The same might be said of the more than 50,000 people who die (directly or indirectly) because of alcohol each year. All

*handling emotions*

summer we practiced different exercises that would help us (and also patients or students) to master negative feelings. While most of them would make poor reading, they worked. For instance, after an enraging or frustrating event, one could stop long enough to inspect one's behavior, and ask, Am *I* that rage? "Make a model of the feeling," Rinpoche said, "so you can cook it, boil it, eat it." Sometimes we meditated on a negative emotion at the time it happened, trying to see it with a relaxed mind, free of concepts, watching the energy. Several people were surprised to realize how much they enjoyed their anger, and how little they really wanted to change. The architect in our midst said he would look at negative feelings until they became neutral. By the end of the summer he felt he was no longer controlled by his feelings, but that he had the control: "I don't have to waste my energy jumping into emotional situations and reacting negatively."

Detachment, a central concept in Buddhism, is largely misunderstood in the West. It is not detachment from life, but from the

*detachment from conditionings*

conditioned hangups we consider normal. We accept competition, avarice, and deceit normal in personal and economic life, yet strangely enough we never consider that they have consequences for health. Therapists must treat individuals who live in a world of Watergate and corporate connivance, yet traditionally we consider health beyond the domain of morality. Thus in the Buddhist view, we can never go to the source of our problems, be they drug addiction, alcoholism, or neurosis. One can see how moral conflicts could create illness. In the so-called socialization process, a child is encouraged to utter small lies. At first the falsity may be accompanied by a felt tension. After many repetitions, it may become subliminal. Finally, in adulthood, the person may catch his breath before speaking, and suffer from the respiratory ailments of shallow breathers. The consequences of one's actions are expressed in the idea of *karma*, a word that is used faddishly today, but which implies the principle that good begets good, and evil, evil. Because of our cultural conditioning, however, we no longer see these chains of action and reaction in our lives.

All summer Rinpoche gave us simple, straight-forward exercises

*reversing habits*

in reversing stereotyped habits. These showed us how our most inconspicuous habits were affecting us. "Don't say 'yes' for a week," he instructed. This makes embarrassingly clear the amount of time and energy spent daily on hypocrisy, assenting to be nice, or from habit. He asked us to be silent for a weekend. We create friction and dissipate our

energies in needless talk. Silence can heal agitated patients, he said, and periods of silence at meals or during the evening might be an emollient to disharmonious families. For example, paying attention to posture or sitting, or using the left hand if one is right handed, all stimulate one to the kind of mindfulness that is essential to Buddhist development. As one begins to notice how many aspects of one's character, posture, body vitality and mental habits there are to watch, then it is plain why enlightenment is considered the job of a lifetime, or perhaps many lifetimes.

Along with a vast number of simple, and direct exercises that would show us to ourselves—like looking into a mirror—if we took the trouble to do them, there were several meditations on which Rinpoche placed particular emphasis. One required our concentrating single-pointedly at the reflection of our eyes in a mirror for three hours at a stretch, or until we had done it for twenty-four hours. *looking into a mirror*

A garbage truck was grinding outside our dimly lit classroom, and I recall looking around at the dismayed faces, as Rinpoche added this assignment. Some of the local participants were still holding office hours for patients, or had prior commitments for evenings. It was getting to be a choice between homework and sleep. In Tibet, a student fortunate enough to hear his teaching would have followed Rinpoche's instructions to the letter whatever the cost. But we had not completed our twenty-four hours by the end of the week. Rinpoche was beginning to see that our commitment to learning was not undivided, and that we were busy even when we considered ourselves to be free. If he was privately perplexed or disappointed, he adroitly turned unaccomplished

written assignments into group discussions. We could not fully appreciate the uniqueness of our curriculum: it was so condensed that we were to attempt, in twenty-four hours, what a Tibetan might have done for six months. Still, six hours of meditation in a day seemed infinite to me.

*projections*

I sat before the mirror, expecting nothing, watching my monkey face watch me. I had envied others who saw visions, experienced telepathy, or other psychic phenomena, or easily entered deep hypnotic trances. My scientific skepticism, perhaps, had kept me so anchored to earth that I doubted I would ever enjoy the magical or transcendent experiences others seemed to enter so easily. Suddenly, the face I had believed to be my own looked at me with an expression so alien and inhuman that I gasped audibly. When the fear abated, I saw that the face was quite old, wizened. It looked dead. Suddenly it became a child looking at me with candid curiosity. Faces came toward me in a procession, some of them familiar, my mother, an uncle, a Mongol with cruel features, a medieval abbess, a catlike Burmese, my death-mask, people who might have been the grandparents I had never known, and among them a dark brown chimpanzee. I watched, not conscious of any emotion, and at some point the mirror darkened and went black. My eyes were open but I saw nothing! This, as I later learned, was a common experience when people truly quieted their minds. It did not last. In a few seconds, the procession of faces resumed, and at some point a region between the eyes began to sparkle like a strobe. Then, perhaps in surprise, or fear, I felt disoriented in space, as if I were falling. I was . . . my face touched the mirror.

Each of us had projected our own fear, self-disapproval or infatuation, anger, or some other distortion onto the image in the mirror, projections that we saw visually. However, when we achieved a state of emptiness, without thoughts and projections, the images —including that of our own face—would vanish.

Rinpoche listened benignly, drawing out some reticent or shy members, pointedly leaving others alone. He had an uncanny way of knowing where we were at, even if we didn't speak.

On a grey morning, he would sometimes make a motion in the air as if to cut the fog in our heads. He would abruptly have us stand. "Bend and touch the floor," he commanded. "Bend back. Now close your eyes. What color do you see?" He went around the room. People certainly saw different parts of the spectrum. Most of us would have dismissed a splash of color in our visual field as not worth noting. But Rinpoche was interested. From these traces he seemed to be measuring something about our consciousness, as if it were familiar territory. It was awesome to realize that a Tibetan teacher would understand the private signs of inner events as though they were written on a map. Nothing was dismissed. A color, a sensation, was significant: it told where our minds were in their evolution to greater refinement.

*map of consciousness*

In response to his question about color, one man who had been sitting skeptically in the back replied, "Blue." "Ah, blue. The color of Buddhahood, serenity," Rinpoche remarked, quickly adding, "and also of ignorance, stupidity." Self-congratulation was punctured as fast as it arose, and competing for praise was a self-defeating effort. The moment a person perfected a yoga position, Rinpoche would praise and push in the same sentence. "That's very good—now hold it for two minutes," he would say as the person gasped to his limit. Every day we added to our repertoire of Tibetan Yoga positions, some of which resembled isometrics. While some of these were unfamiliar, they had the familiar purpose of enhancing mental and physical awareness, improving muscle tone, and balance and concentration.

Rinpoche's instruction in diagnosis involved sitting in front of a person in a state of emptiness, observing without words or barriers everything about them. Professional questionnaires and scientific evaluations are often a substitute for close observation, a skill that is rarely explicitly trained even in medical schools. Moreover, it is a skill that would be useless without emptying the mind, for our ceaseless mental activity, biases, and preconceptions would filter out important information. Even when we think ourselves quiet, there is some mental noise occluding perception. Anyone who wants to see this for himself

*close observation*

can perform a test that Rinpoche gave. He said, "Count all your thoughts for an hour." This meant all thoughts, images, sensations, sounds, feelings—anything you are aware of. (My own count was over 1,000.)

*chakras*

Some breathing exercises we were introduced to are practiced to open up crucial nodes, known as *chakras*. According to the yoga teachings of the Near and Far East since about the sixth century B.C., and the theory of acupuncturists, the center of energy is the cerebro-spinal axis of the spinal column and brain. The chakras correspond roughly to nerve foci that control body functioning and the endocrine system. At the base of the spine is the chakra of reproductive energy, the famous kundalini energy. The aim of many exercises is to release this energy toward the chakras of the solar plexus, the heart, throat, third eye, and crown. Without knowing it, most people have seen designs of the chakra system in the central geometrics of oriental rugs. Many Christian saints in the brass reliefs of the eleventh and twelfth centuries have a diamond or other design on the forehead between the eyebrows at the point known as the chakra of superconsciousness, or psychic center. In addition to representing centers for internal functioning, the chakras also represent receivers for cosmic energies and geomagnetic changes. We were hoping that our breathing exercise would allow us to channel energy, open spinal chakras, and perhaps remove our blocks to higher awareness.

*breathing exercises*

In actuality, the first breathing sessions sounded more like a ward of gasping emphysemics. Rinpoche, calmly seated with his colorful striped quilt over his legs, told us to take off sweaters, despite the dampness and chill in the room. With repetition of the exercise, the nature of the experience changed. A man reported an opening in the region of his heart. A few people felt energy crawling up the spine, and found their heads filled with brilliant light. Claudio Naranjo said, "This is a most important exercise for me. I had the sensation of being born anew into many states of consciousness I never experienced before." Yet he confessed that he feared for his life each breath, positive he would never make it back alive. I, too, felt that fear, despite a peculiar tranquility as if my body were a mere anchor. One of the problems of unsupervised practice of these breathing exercises is that people can unwittingly do themselves damage, and incite startling changes in consciousness that they cannot handle alone.

*meditation*

We began almost every afternoon with chanting, creating a human ocean of sound that can arouse strangely primordial feelings. Americans, Rinpoche noticed, seemed particularly susceptible to chanting, and would rapidly create fellow-feeling in this way, or a transition from ordinary conversation to the stillness of meditation.

Ability to meditate varied in the group. My own, still at the neanderthal level, often left me wishing I could stop thoughts, sneeze without disturbing the group, scratch or conquer numbness and pain in my legs. If the ache and thoughts evaporated for a few moments I would be so overjoyed and proud of my momentary stillness that I would end it with what the Buddhists call grasping. The paradox of meditation, like relaxation, is that one must maintain it without making an effort. My efforts not to make an effort usually plunged me into a yet more primitive state—drowsiness. Prior to this course I might have described myself as energetic, but profound laziness began to show itself as we proceeded to the more demanding meditations.

Analytical meditation was one of the basic tools for self-under-standing, by directly inspecting the nature of inner experience without words or metaphors. If we heard a sound we were to begin by inquir-ing, "Who heard the sound?" and to look within for the hearing part of ourselves. Then we were to ask, "Who is looking at he who hears?" and "Who is observing the observer?" None of this questioning was intellectual, but wordless. For many people it became a regression, as endless as a hall of mirrors. Some responded with a characteristic violence, seeing their past self-images with pain and longing to escape, feeling as though they were burning. The products of this kind of inward look are undramatic, but they were substantial for each person. An articulate Italian professor discovered that his so-called random thoughts were not random: they were the cravings of different parts of himself, and he could trace the origins of each "random" thought in this meditation. *self-understanding*

A few people found that the procedure led to a loss of their sense of identity, extremely frightening for a Westerner, although it is desirable in Buddhist development. We had begun to ask questions about our own nature that we had probably not asked since adoles-cence, the questions of children before they are frustrated and turned off by cultural indifference. Who am I? *Where* is the entity called a self? Is it possible I don't exist—that there is only an awareness encrusted by concepts of self and ego? Is it possible that this awareness could function in its body without any need for a personality? *who am I?*

During our first meetings, Rinpoche had innocently asked, "What is a thought?" Our replies had come from books and teachers, external responses that would not be considered knowledge by a Buddhist, for knowledge must be felt. By mid-July we were beginning to analyze a thought by a mapping that is uniquely *Nyingma*, a system that has been validated over the centuries.

In the momentary blankness between thoughts, which appears to be so fleeting to us, the Nyingma lamas have mapped at least nine discrete conscious states. Like the Eskimos with their more than twenty words for snow, these nuances of experience have inspired a sizable vocabulary and take very fine tuning to detect. Needless to say, this interior cartography cannot be taught by books, but requires the guidance and feedback of a teacher.

*the*
*ground*
*state*

The ground state between thoughts, ever present in varying density, has been called *kun-gzhi*. Like gravity, it has many gradations and may be experienced as heavier or lighter, but so long as one remains in an earthly consciousness, it is present. The heavier *kun-gzhi* is a densely peaceful state, experienced briefly by athletes after a maximum exertion, a blankness experienced after deep breathing exercises or orgasm. It resembles inebriation, and it could, indeed, be used to help an alcoholic or drug-addicted person, since it is a state they seek. For instance by running up and down hill for 25 minutes, or doing a strenuous exercise, they could perhaps be taught to induce this state. Once having learned the feeling, they could be taught how to attain and perpetuate the serenity without drugs.

We would do an exercise to induce the oceanic blankness of *kun-gzhi*, and then like fishermen awaiting a nibble, we would await a flicker of energy, a distant harbinger of a movement that could become a thought in the back of the head. It might stir like a barely perceived breeze or light, a distant restlessness that was called *kun-gzhi nam-shes*. Soon after, one might feel a sense of identification as if the perception were one's own, a subtle discrimination—a state labeled as *nun yid*.

We were beginning to inspect the processes that Westerners call the unconscious. In many of our exercises we had been getting ready to train our sight on the terrain that is a forbidden no-man's-land according to Western psychology. The conscious mind does not sit and stare at the workings of the unconscious, according to post-Freudian understanding. Yet we were doing precisely this. The presumption that a part of our consciousness is inaccessible—is unconscious—may be based mainly on Western habits. We rarely sit still and observe our minds. Moreover, we have nobody to teach us how to watch our processes. Mental events seem mercurial and too rapid to watch in ordinary consciousness. It had taken us many weeks of intensive daily training before we could slow down our thoughts enough, and sharpen our awareness so that we could begin to observe and identify the many kinds of events between one thought and another—watching the "unconscious" at work.

*the*
*unconscious*

Tibetan Buddhist theory, which is comprehensive beyond our expectations of a psychological theory, depends upon much direct observation, and presumes extensive mental training. Tibetans have a metaphor for the untrained mind: a one-armed rider on a blind wild horse.

The rampant quality of that restless, untrained mind is evident in our pathology, and in our relative neglect of introspection. In the

last ten years, a few Western scientists like Dr. Joe Kamiya, in San Francisco, or Dr. Elmer Green, at The Menninger Foundation, have been trying to correlate inner experience with EEG (Electroenceph-alogram) tracings, in order to construct a matrix and vocabulary for introspective experience. EEG is a limited instrument (because of the limits of the machines of the 1930s, we study only the brainwave frequencies between 1–50 CPS, although there are brainwave changes occuring in thousands of cycles per second); nonetheless it may be fruitful to match the subtle Tibetan mapping with EEG tracings—once a scientist interested in this problem has himself learned the Tibetan cartography of consciousness. To be given a glimpse of a well-devel-oped inner language and technique for watching the "unconscious" is extraordinary enough, but in addition we were given access to sleep and dreaming in a way that is also beyond the inquiry of the waking mind.

Most of our emotional associations are created haphazardly, and, for the most part, we do not know why we react to a particular color. Indeed we usually don't know what aspects of our environment trigger our feelings. It became apparent that the boundaries between one's self and the outside world depends on our conscious habits of maintaining fixed perception patterns. Throughout the summer we had cultivated certain images in order to construct deliberate associations and desired emotional states that could be produced at will.

There were certainly personal changes during the eight-week summer session: a physician, Michael Smith, spoke for many when he observed that he had become more patient and able to concentrate. Several people felt they had accomplished what therapy or prior psychoanalysis had failed to do—gaining control over their emotions and discovering that they had a choice of how they would react. Many people expressed greater ease and tranquility as a result. (One woman emphasized that her tranquility was not fragile, but that she remained serene even in the midst of a family crisis in which her mother had nearly died.) During the summer we had occasionally stopped to assay changes in consciousness. Some people were sleeping less. Others were noticing a sensory brilliance, as if the world were suffused with the clear colors of childhood, and a return to sensory innocence. One social worker from New Jersey remarked that he had tested his consciousness by trying to flip a coin and predict the outcome. With eyes closed he flipped, and guessed correctly the first time. He tried again, and again he was right. After being right nine times in a row he quit. Rinpoche was much amused. "Maybe he should go to the racetrack," he said.

Some of the effects which required the cloistered intensity of the training period, might have been attributed to the lack of noise and busyness of everyday life, but two months later, lives were changing.

Claudio Naranjo found himself thrust into a period of solitary work, a retreat. Reverend Tilden Edwards of the Episcopal Diocese in Washington, D. C. was ebullient with a new inner freedom and deepened sense of compassion. He is Director of the Ecumenical Training Center in Washington, and since his return he has found himself leaning less heavily on behavioral science for therapy, and more on meditation. Following the Buddhist program, which ended in late August, Rev. Edwards went to a week-long Jesuit retreat. His understanding of the Christian saints had deepened. "I often found myself thinking, that is just what Rinpoche told us, as I read them: now I feel I can express and share their religious experience far more deeply." At the level of deep mystical experience there is really not much difference between the Christian and the Buddhist saint, but direct experience is precisely what has been missing from most of the Christian churches for many years, and this is where meditation training may have a considerable impact in reviving religious experience.

People look for external changes. Professor Donald Michael seemed lighter to his friends, who told him that he had lost weight, which he hadn't—at least not physical weight. He found that he was looking at his life in new perspective, and that it was becoming lighter, less complicated. "I find myself simplifying," he said. "For instance, by October I usually have 10–15 speaking engagements lined up. But I began asking myself why I was speaking." Prestige, importance, he decided, no longer interested him. Speaking engagements and endless committees used to complicate his life. "I do ask myself whether I'm copping out, whether I am judging the value of things correctly . . . but even that question has more meaning now. I never enjoyed cognitive thinking so much before." *external changes*

Many students felt that the most important experience of the eight weeks was Rinpoche himself. "He represents a different ideal of what a fully realized human being can become." He has qualities of rootedness, a childlike joy and curiosity, and a kind of cosmic noblesse oblige. Rinpoche's profound mastery and knowledge of the use of psychic energies gave him an awesome quality, and we were aware of the immensity and unfamiliarity of his universe. *Rinpoche himself*

Everyone knew that in eight weeks we would only scratch the surface of the Nyingma psychology. Today it is painfully clear that there is only one way of learning the comprehensive psychological skills—it is essential to have a guide. Only by deeply studying with the lamas of the Nyingma tradition will we ever have a glimmering idea of the scope of their work. ❖

# PRACTICE IS:

Living our daily life
dedicating our daily meals to all sentient beings
seeing golden light of each day with new eyes
relaxing—nothing you do is that important
sharing with others the blessings received
Being with Awareness
cutting through ego
letting the senses slip away
loving with compassion
expanding
eternally suspending time and space
increasingly surren-daring to Isness
Knowing
practicing
joining the dance—exquisite movement of what Is
listening—allowing sounds to enter as friends
hearing the silence
flowing with the eternal river
melting
being willing for nothing to happen
seeing the universe within the blossom
dying and being born with each breath
Being in Union
Being without "attachment to Samsara or Nirvana"

# sKum Nye Relaxation

*The meditative concentration of the Bodhisattva is
(1) devoid of all dichotomy; (2) produces relaxation of
tension in the mind and its functions; (3) is completely
tranquil; (4) without arrogance or (5) emotional
evaluation; and (6) is devoid of all characteristics.
By this one lives happily in this present life.*

BODHISATTVABHŪMI

FOR ME, THE practice and application of Tibetan Buddhism is twofold:
practice, and the teaching or passing on of practices to others. Only through
my own experience and subsequent understanding is it possible to teach
others. And the beauty here is not in 'teaching,' but rather in being able to
share with others a whole series of spaces and realms that are available to all of
us. To the degree that ego can step aside and let the teachings pass through, we
all are channels.

One of the basic and essential secrets within the practice of meditation is
*sKum Nye* relaxation. This is a Tibetan approach of attaining a most deep
state of peace and tranquility through various exercises. The foundation of
awareness is found in stillness, stillness where our body and our mind are one.

AUBREY LINDGREN is a teacher of transpersonal psychology in Berkeley, California,
and participated in the summer 1973 Training Program at the Nyingma Institute. A Tibetan
method of physical relaxation and meditation, *sKum Nye*, was one of the therapeutic practices
taught during the summer program and was particularly useful in releasing the many stresses
and tensions of contemporary life. Ms. Lindgren now instructs the continuing class in *sKum
Nye* at the Institute.

Through deep relaxation we gradually let go of the duality of body-mind, experiencing in a simple way that we are whole. We first bring people into the here and now, using breathing, voice, body, and self-awareness. It is most crucial that all five senses are functioning harmoniously and are balanced for the person to appreciate his true and natural state of being. We need to be thoroughly present to ourselves, and develop a love for ourselves that is harmonious—a union of mind, body, feeling, and perception. We then begin to move into a realm of direct state of awareness as concepts and judgments are gradually displaced. Deep stillness, quiet, physical and mental peace, are necessary to touch direct experience which does not travel into the brain and become translated into a cognition. In *sKum Nye* we spend much attention developing the senses, deepening and widening the subtleties of our feelings, and moving into tranquility and blissful spaces. *sKum Nye* is a process of refining and loving ourselves—until we are able to move beyond self-image and beyond the senses.

For Westerners, especially, the notion that relaxation means more than taking a vacation or going to a movie, comes as a surprise. *sKum Nye* is more than the level of relaxation which growth centers present as sensitivity awareness or deep massage. *sKum Nye* helps to bring about an understanding that our final refuge is our own consciousness, that within us all lies our best friend, our lover, our home, our family, our guru, waiting to unfold and be revealed. The process, according to Rinpoche's teaching, uses various exercises, visualizations and asanas.

Self-massage can be done prior to sitting or just about anywhere in your daily life. It can be very pleasing and relaxing, just as much as when you are receiving a massage from another. In self-massage we are aiding the circulation of blood, oxygen, and energy throughout the entire system. We also utilize specific pressure points as a means to balance our body and breathing. We work on the premise that within the body are emotional memories which we cling to in the form of body blocks or tightness, and later this becomes even more encased by protective layers of muscles. So through massage we are able to release this tension which has produced much anxiety and also to release the flow of vital energy within the entire organism. What was excruciating pain turns to flowing relief. It is also an opportunity for the inner observer to carefully watch the contents of his own psyche passing before him and to not become caught in its drama. Here we are developing an aspect of ourself which is like a witness rather than a victim of our own ego.

These asanas or yogic postures have been passed down through many generations of Tibetan teachers and affect an individual on several levels. One level invokes the emotional tenor of the specific asana, while the pure posture, or mudra of this ancient tradition connects one with a deep source of natural tranquility. As *sKum Nye* deeply affects the muscles and nervous system, it is necessary to maintain inner concentration, discipline and balance. This brings one strongly into the here and now. During and after these specific exercises we

are more able to observe the raw material of our consciousness and may enter into one of the many levels of *kun-gzhi*, the foundation of all consciousness. Within *kun-gzhi*, we rest in a space which is prior to any concept of self-image, prior to separating the world into a subject, or I, and an object, or you. In this space awareness is both cultivated and sustained.

Once true, deep relaxation comes, our mind reflects this stillness. We are able to contemplate, as beginners, and may investigate the space between the thoughts. We can discover the multi-level sound track inside us. Many thoughts occur within the space of several seconds. One thought may be beginning while another is in the middle of its process. As we still the mind, these tracks slowly disappear, and we find the moment where there is no thought. If we suspend commenting upon there being no thought—when there is nobody doing the thinking—we let go of our separateness from all that is. We move into a pre-cognitive and pre-verbal level that is also pre-self-image.

Here we are at the early juncture of the illusion that 'I' exist as separate from the object. It is most necessary to directly know this meditative space of consciousness for any further practice.

As a 'transpersonal psychologist' working with people, one of my directions of focus is to create a bridge between the Western problem-orientation of psychology and the Eastern concern with Being. We all have peak experiences which are but tastes of spaces we could live in much more consistently. The question then becomes one of integration, of inclusion. We need to help people relax to the point where Being shines through the layers of ego, and where ego is less the dictator of our lives. Once a person can be at rest, then his clinging to private problems loosens and his problems slip away. At first it is difficult for people to give up their suffering, their problems. They are attached to believing that difficulties exist and are important. Further, they believe that they *are* their problems. Here I am referring mostly to problems, fantasies and fears, which are generated within our minds—not actual situations such as starvation. So much of what we identify as problems are really a matter of perspective, which we then compound. We need to identify what is our conditioning that generates these perspectives, or ego, and what is Being or essence. Westerners have found a pseudo-satisfaction in mulling over their emotional problems. We have found this nourishing, as witnessed by all the therapy-oriented groups. Yet, when examined, we actually become more trapped in our greedy, craving nature. We are insatiable in our search for more love—a kind of giving in order to get. In turning to meditation there comes a nourishment which is much more subtly penetrating, more full and encompassing, flowing into all aspects of our lives. As we begin to open ourselves to a more spontaneous 'balance,' there is nourishment in abundance, a quality of nectar and honey. The world about us begins to have a lustrous sheen upon everything.

As a result of meditation, our consciousness—perceptions and conceptions—begins to change: at first, gradually, then in a more masterful, subtle manner, as a painter paying heed with a most delicate brush to the details of his creation. The foundation or basic material from which emotions arise becomes more tranquil and smooth, as a deep pool is quiet within the forest. There is less and less about which we become excited or agitated. There is more equanimity or acceptance—an acceptance which is not a giving up in hopelessness, but rather an acceptance that truly appreciates the exquisiteness of what Is. And there is detachment—not a denial of feelings, but rather feelings with a slightly different tonal nature—compassion without the drama of sympathy, and an understanding that comes from really having lived that trip, whatever the trip may be. Detachment comes with an awareness of the cycles of emotions within us which are our own traps of illusion. As the world in the immediate moment begins to sparkle, we begin to see and appreciate the events and timing of what Is within our own lives. Our desires loosen and we become filled with an increasing satisfaction in just Being. Ego slips, Being nourishes us, and we open.

This process of awakening comes with meditation. Awakening, on various levels, reveals to us how much our 'reality' is a result of opinions, judgments, interpretations, and conditioning. We discover we are rarely living our life in the moment of its occurring. We are too busy thinking about the past or future to be present in the here and now. We also awaken on a physiological level: for our physical body is a gross covering for more subtle energy bodies. One of these is the *chakra* system. The opening and activity of the chakras can be stimulated through the pressure-point system of *sKum Nye* massage, and through meditation, music, and concentration. These points are real centers within our body. Often, with the awakening of these centers, we experience a localized pressure, pulsation, energy rippling, tingling, or heat. Our emotions reflect this process as well, while our perceptions alter gradually–for example, seeing more light or the movement of energy within space. Our dreams, or lack of them, also indicate subtle transformations: our whole sleep pattern for example, is subject to change. The energies released by *sKum Nye* exercises and meditation practices are finally beyond words, and only direct experience with them can reveal the amazing beauty that is within us.

With deep appreciation and gratitude I wish to thank the guru, Tarthang Tulku, Rinpoche, for his help and compassion which is helping me to map the infinite realms of my own consciousness. ❖

PART THREE

# PHILOSOPHY

# Mind and Feelings

*In its true state, mind is naked, immaculate,*
*not made of anything, being of the Voidness,*
*clear, vacuous, without duality, transparent,*
*timeless, uncompounded, unimpeded, colorless,*
*not realizable as a separate thing, but as the*
*unity of all things, yet not composed of them,*
*of one taste, and transcendent over differentiation.*

PADMA SAMBHAVA

As HUMAN BEINGS, it is very important that we have feelings. Sometimes it is difficult for us to understand our own mind or consciousness, but our mind and body feelings are familiar to us and are always available. In general, there are three types of feelings. The first are positive: happy, joyful, balanced feelings. The second are negative: irritated, frustrated or very restless feelings—a kind of uncomfortableness. The third kind are neither positive nor negative, but kind of neutral and dull: nothing is happening. These are the three types of feelings.

*develop a balanced attitude*

In our lives it is important for positive feelings to develop. The negative residues and on-going emotional turbulence of each day can all be used to develop a clear, balanced, positive attitude. The question is, how do we use each situation? Normally, feelings divide us: this is a good feeling, this is a bad feeling. Like mail which goes to many different countries, the mind distributes our thoughts and feelings in different directions. But first, for positive feelings to grow, we need to develop our mind. Feelings generally control us: we "follow our feelings," but often we are like blind men crossing a busy street. Before feelings take over, we can examine our mental attitudes and see that they develop in a positive way.

Where then is mind? In each immediate experience, the mind presents itself as energy. Mind has no particular form. The mind is like 'empty space' that can adopt many different forms. Without space, we cannot make shape, color, or form. Without space, nothing can exist. So mind as space is really a continuum, but it is not solid. Mind in its emptiness, mind-nature, is like empty light—or a crystal in which all things reflect.

*mind is like empty space*

All feelings arise from the mind, which in its spaciousness is like the ocean; yet mind is empty. Labeling or naming what mind is, results in thoughts, perceptions, and concepts. Mind-nature, or self-nature, has no position, no characteristics. Mind is not a thing. Mind is not a substance. It has no form, no color, no beginning. Mind does not go anywhere. Mind is not an entity. It does not belong to 'any,' or 'one,' or 'a,' or 'the.' Mind is not something individual. Mind has no parents.

*mind has no parents*

As individuals, we say that all sorts of things affect us, that we are conditioned. But actually, our ego or self-image determines our conditioning. Like carpenters, we tend to 'shape' our minds, and each of us can shape our mind in a completely different way. We do this mainly by labeling and forming different concepts. In this way we continue to develop Samsara which, we may say, follows an evolutionary form.

The more we come to understand what 'mind' is, the more rapidly our conception of 'mind' changes. At first we may think we understand mind, but later, our concepts and labels change. This must be dealt with at an experiential level. If we say mind is a certain way, then where do we come from? Should we not have some 'from,' some origin? We are not necessarily looking for scientific answers, but for practical, effective answers with which to involve ourselves. We want to know these answers, not in a purely intellectual way, just in our heads, but according to how we actually 'feel.'

*the origin of mind*

We may ask, are feelings possible without mind? Can we at the same time deny 'mind' and accept 'feelings'? Or can we say they are the same? We do not need a laboratory to test these things. Our laboratory is here within us. Through our own direct experience we can find these answers for ourselves. ❖

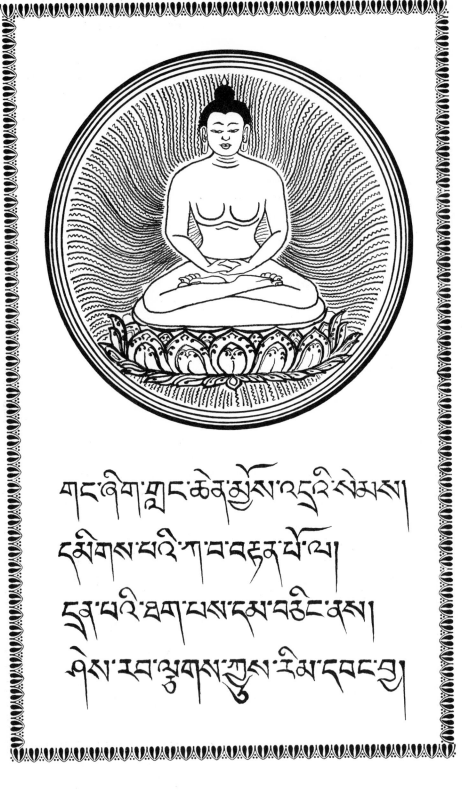

གང་ཞིག་སྐྱབ་ཆེན་སྒྱིས་འདུའི་སེམས། །

འབྲེགས་པའི་ག་བ་བརྟན་པོ་ལ། །

ཐུབ་པའི་ཞག་པས་ལམ་བཅིང་ནས། །

ཞེས་རབ་ལྕགས་ཀྱུས་ཅིག་འབང་རྒྱུ། །

*Firmly tie the mind resembling a mad elephant*
*To the strong pillar of its perceptual content*
*With the rope of contemplative inspection*
*And gradually tame it with the hook*
        *of discrimination.*

*Let the deceptive appearances subside in the sphere*
        *that is wholly positive,*
*Since all that ceaselessly appears*
        *as manifested creativeness*
*Out of the unchanging ground of the absolute real*
*Is the indivisibility of the continuum of reality*
        *and its intrinsic awareness.*

གཞི་དབྱིངས་འགྱུར་བ་མེད་པ་ལས། །

རྩལ་སྣང་འགགས་མེད་སྟུང་རྩ་ཀུན། །

དབྱིངས་དང་རིག་པ་དབྱེར་མེད་པས། །

འཁྲུལ་སྣང་ཀུན་བཟང་ཀློང་དུ་ཐིམ། །

# Early Forms of
# Tibetan Buddhism

*As the ancient Buddhas seized the Thought of
Enlightenment, in like manner they followed regularly
on the path of Bodhisattva instruction. Thus also
do I use the Thought of Enlightenment to arise
for the welfare of the world, and thus shall I
practice these instructions in proper order.*

ŚĀNTIDEVA

THE TERMS rNYINGMA, 'old,' and rNyingmapa, 'follower of the old
translated texts,' were used after the eleventh century when Rin-chen bZang-
po (958–1055) initiated a new technique of translating which was based on a
very exact analysis of the terms in the Sanskrit originals available at the time.
Many of these original sources have been lost in the course of time and we have
them today only in their excellent Tibetan translations. The technique was
such that the Sanskrit words were analyzed according to their roots, prefixes
and various endings. Most significantly, the various prefixes which gave shades
of meanings to the use of the words were now standardized in the translations.
It was a procedure by which one could now be very exact as far as the original
wording was concerned, but it also was a rather mechanical form of matching
the Indian word with and incorporating it into the Tibetan language. Later on,
the objection was raised (by those opposing this method) that the new

---

HERBERT V. GUENTHER holds Ph.D. degrees from the universities of Munich and
Vienna, and is chairman of the Department of Far East Studies at the University of
Saskatchewan. A well-known historian, scholar and translator, Dr. Guenther has published
several important books on Tibetan Buddhism, including *The Royal Song of Saraha*, *Treasures
on the Tibetan Middle Way*, *The Jewel Ornament of Liberation*, and *The Tantric View of Life*.

translations had lost much of the original flavour and the spirit which had made the texts so acceptable.

These newly translated works were collected into the huge collections of the Kanjur, which is said to contain the words of the Buddha, and the Tanjur, containing the translations of commentaries on and explanations of the Buddha-word. Unfortunately, all the works belonging to the earlier tradition were excluded. Consequently we know very little (at least in the Western world) about the early tradition and the early form of Buddhist thought in Tibet. Moreover, a tendency arose to claim as the authentic form of Buddhism only the development of Buddhist thought that was reflected in works of which a Sanskrit or other Indian language original had been available, which in practice meant that everything non-Indian was no longer recognized as 'Buddhistic.' The tendency to shut off the rNyingma tradition, although it is still very much alive, has continued into modern times.

The tradition emphasizing the Indian form did not take into account that much of what had happened in India had been a new development and had very scanty connections with what one would call the original form. But since it came from India it was automatically considered to be the proper way and everything else was ignored.

Historians of Tibet (like many historians) were absolute falsifiers of facts. Having a bias for their particular point of view, they wrote Tibetan history in a way which makes Tibet appear as uncouth and savage, and they continued saying that there was no civilization in Tibet before Buddhism came.

Official history dates the development of Tibet as 557. However, in 632, the minister Thu-mi-sambhota, under the first religious king Srong-btsen-sgam-po, had gone to Kashmir to study grammar and he had modeled his Tibetan grammar on the available works of Panini and Chandragomin—two very famous Sanskrit grammarians who had practically anticipated modern linguistics. In 655 the ancient annals of Tun-huang record that "the text of the Dharma was written." It is rather surprising that it took only twenty years for the Tibetans to learn their own language and immediately to proceed to the very difficult work of translating texts which by nature are very abstruse. Since the capacity of translating a complex and subtle system of ideas presupposes an equivalent high standard of literacy and cultural awareness, it is obvious that the official history is rather misleading. All that can be stated with certainty is that before Buddhism was officially recognized, it had already had a long, long antecedent, and Buddhist ideas were present in the general cultural setting.

The geographical situation of Tibet has always been such that it was surrounded by countries which long before 632 had come under the influence of ideas from various regions—from the West, Southwest, and particularly from the Southeast. The possibility that Buddhist ideas had been available in Tibet before their official recognition is greatly supported by Tibet's geographic situation.

There was the rather mythical kingdom, Zhang-Zhung in the region about the Kailas mountain, which is described in Bardic poetry as a kind of wild country with wild horses. Chinese princesses complained that for political reasons they had to marry the rulers there and they felt unhappy in this wilderness. Actually, Zhang-Zhung had an extensive literature which at this time is still waiting to be deciphered as the language is not yet known.

Toward the West were Iran, Kashmir, Ladakh, and Afghanistan, which had long before come under Indian influence, and certainly Buddhist ideas were already there. We have very few texts dating back to this time because it was not the custom to preserve a tradition in writing. The tradition in the East has always been one of oral transmission. Knowledge was committed to memory, and only when unstable conditions presented a danger that the tradition might be lost were things written down. Only in times of upheaval did people try to preserve their knowledge in writing. Therefore in Asia the first date at which something is committed to writing is not necessarily the date at which the work actually originated. A new era started when the so-called 'religious kings' consolidated the land which they ruled and which then became known as Tibet.

Because of the geographical situation in Tibet, wherever we look we find that communication has come from all sides, but the trend has been to consider it as having come from India alone. It could just as well have been (and I think future research will show) that India was not always the source of knowledge but was also on the receiving end.

With this changed attitude in outlook we can hypothetically date the beginning of Buddhism in Tibet as having taken place before the year 632 and the reign of the religious kings, which marks the time Tibet entered history (in the sense that we understand it) as a great power. At the same time, China again reemerged as a power by acquiring a new dynasty, the T'ang (618–906). However, between 665 and 666, Khotan, Kucha, Karashahr, and Kashgar fell under Tibetan domination. Khotan and Kucha had long been important seats of Buddhist thought. In Kucha the Hinayāna form of Buddhism was predominant while in Khotan it was the Mahāyāna form. These two forms were equally important for Tibet and for China.

The first literary documents seem to be closely connected with the Hinayāna, as much of their contents deals with discipline and also with meditational techniques. Often what we call 'meditation' has been used as a means of escape rather than as a means towards integration and finding oneself. When things become difficult, people try to find a solution by looking *outward* when the answer could better be found by looking *inward*. In order to practice meditation one has to have guidelines. The first texts translated (we don't have the Sanskrit originals) were word lists or guidelines for meditation. These were the earliest translations and they are still found in the Chinese form of Buddhism which came via Kucha and Khotan. These lists of terms describe phenomena that occur while practicing meditation.

*Guru Padma Sambhava; the most important teacher in all of Nyingma history, through whom all lineages trace their origin*

*Thang-tong Gyalpo, famous Nyingma yogi, terton, and bridge-builder who founded Derge Monastery*

Together with these word lists there are certain numerical instructions. The interesting point is that these lists are not only preserved in China; we also find them with the very early rNyingmapa representatives. This pushes the introduction of Buddhism into Tibet back much earlier than we had previously thought.

Another important historical point that contradicts the Tibetan tradition about themselves as "stupid and barbarious," is the succession of Tao An (312–385) by his disciple Tan-i as abbot of the important Ch'ang-sha monastery at Chiang-ling. He is said to have been a Ch'iang; this term indicates one of the tribes of the proto-Tibetan stock. The fact that a 'Tibetan' became abbot of a center of learning and was noted for his erudition shows that Buddhist ideas had, at least among the educated people, been accepted more than three hundred years before tradition claims Buddhism to have come to Tibet. Obviously a person not well versed in the subject matter could not have risen to such an important post as the abbot of a monastery. The account of Tan-i is preserved only in Chinese sources, but we have no reason to doubt their accuracy.

The area around Kucha was dominated by Hinayāna Buddhism which, apart from insisting on disciplines for the life of the layman and the monk, emphasized the use of meditational practices which go back to the earliest forms of Indian Buddhism. On the other hand we have the very important area of Khotan, which in Tibetan sources is referred to as Li Yul. By 600, Khotan had come under Tibetan domination for a brief period. However, much earlier, Buddhism had already been well established there, particularly in its philosophical form which had a strong impact on the East. During this early period, when China was divided and ruled by 'foreign dynasties,' the philosophical form of Buddhism had two specific aspects: one was the tendency to escape, and the other to impress upon the people the importance of either the ruler or of an ideology. The contemporary scene can serve as an illustration. When under stress, people believe that by turning to pietism and by following the rules that are laid down, they may perhaps find salvation. The North of China, in the course of time, developed this pietistic form of Buddhism (so wide-spread today in Japan) which centered around Amitabha. In the South, where the Chinese tradition was much stronger, the interest was more intellectually orientated. Here people were concerned with grasping the meaning of these new ideas which came to them via Khotan.

One of the most important teachings was the so-called Avatamsaka teaching. The Avatamsaka Sutra, as such, is lost in the Sanskrit original and we have only the last section, the Gandavyūha. When recited, it can transpose the listener into a world of light and vibrations. Actually it is the story of the youth Sudhana who asked "How can one find enlightenment?," and is answered by the Bodhisattva Mañjuśri who tells him to set out and learn the proper way; so he is sent on a spiritual quest. Sudhana meets people of all walks of life, merchants, kings, gods, goddesses, and courtesans. Everyone explains that although they have reached a certain stage they still must go further. Sudhana travels on and finally returns to Mañjuśri and finds his answer. This story has found its artistic expression in the famous monument of the Borobudur in Java.

There are names in the Gandavyūha Sutra which point to South India as its origin. Nevertheless the impact of this Sutra has been such that a school developed in Khotan and from there its teachings were brought to China where it became consolidated in the Hua Yen School. From China it went to Korea and Japan where the first Japanese constitution was modeled on the ideas of the Avatamsaka Sutra. We also find many of the ideas that are specific to the Avatamsaka interpretation in the early works of rNyingmapa thinkers. This fact again leads us away from the traditional account to earlier periods when ideas as yet not formalized but in the process of developing were adopted. These ideas were alive and contributed much to the formation of various schools.

During the fourth century, there lived a person whose historicity cannot be doubted and who figures prominently in the rNyingmapa tradition. This person is Shri Singha. The name is Indian, but all sources place his birthplace in Rgya Nag which is the Tibetan name for China. It therefore seems that he was born in an area that was dominated by the Chinese and not by India. As Shri Singha's name is thoroughly Indian, it is a likely hypothesis that he may have belonged to one of the Central Asian people who were made up of various races and national groups that lived there. Certainly, he is one of the more important persons connected with the dissemination of word lists concerning meditation and techniques dealing with certain instructions. About fifteen or sixteen small works are available. (By 'available,' I mean they have been preserved. They are not available in print and it would be difficult to find them on this continent.) Shri Singha's works take Tibetan history back by three hundred years with reference to the official history of Tibet. In 342 Shri Singha is said to have met his teacher posthumously. Here another intriguing factor enters and the beginning of Buddhism in Tibet is again pushed back. His teacher 'Jam-dpal bshes-gnyen had already died and Shri Singha, so the story goes, had a vision of his teacher who had received the teaching from another person. This person was dGa'-rab rdo-rje, an otherwise very elusive figure. We do not know exactly what his name was, but it may have been an Indian name. There are a few works in the Tanjur attributed to Surativajra and the Tibetan for Surativajra is said to have been dGa'rab rdo-rje, although a more 'literal' translation would have been Pramudita-vajra. These works are extremely difficult to understand because of a kind of elliptical style. Their external feature is the emphasis on word lists and the trend toward instructions to proceed in a certain way and arrive at a certain goal. dGa' rab rdo-rje is said to have lived around 52 A.D. This means that at such an early time Buddhists had already come to Tibet. Understood properly, this is to say that Buddhism was in the area known today as Tibet. The introduction of Buddhism is now pushed back approximately six hundred years. From an historical point of view there can be no doubt that these lists of words were the decisive forerunners of what became the early rNyingma tradition.

This tradition continued and in the seventh century a further impetus to the development and growth of Buddhism in Tibet came under Khri-srong lde('u)-btsen. During his reign the Buddhist monk Sāntaraksita and the famous saint Padmasambhāva were invited to Tibet. Padmasambhāva, or reverently Guru Rinpoche, is a very controversial figure from the viewpoint of history. He has written not many, but important, books. One of them is "The Garland of Philosophical Tenets" and begins like all other works of this sort by examining the philosophical schools which had already been formed. The Vaibhāsikas and Sautrāntikas are well represented, but his account of the mentalistic trend is not easily identifiable with what we know from the extant Sanskrit sources. Somehow, if the identification of Padmasambhāva's birthplace in the Swat Valley in Afghanistan is correct, the systematized form of the later philosophical systems had not yet reached that area. Vague ideas were there and Padmasambhāva links them with the older form. When the later Indian systems reached Tibet at a later time, they were more or less outside the old tradition. The rift between the old and the new forms of Buddhism in Tibet is valid only if we look at it in this way. During this period Sino-Tibetan relations were good. But it was the doctrinal anatagonism between the

*J*etsun Senge Wangchuk, the great eleventh century Nyingma lama, who perfected
the precepts of the Dzog Chen Nying Tig. Upholding the direct line from
Vimalamitra, he attained the 'rainbow body' when he passed away.

adherents of Chinese and Indian Buddhism that was to change the total situation with immense repercussions in the political structure. The starting point was the great debate (between 792 and 794) at the monastery of Samye (bsam-yas), where the Indian side was represented by the monk Kamalaśila who had been invited for the occasion, while the Chinese side was represented by the Hoshang (Hwa-shang) Mahāyāna.

As late as the 14th century, kLong-chen rab-'byams-pa states that at Samye those who represented the meditative side and those that represented the intellectual side were highly intelligent persons. He also notes the very important distinction between the Indian side emphasizing the gradual approach to a goal, and the Chinese speaking from the goal—how something looks when we are there. These are quite different viewpoints. The main difference is that with the latter, one speaks from his inner experience, while the former presents an outline of stages to an experience without necessarily having had the decisive experience. There actually is no common meeting ground. This basic difference led to the rift that has continued to this day. The gradual approach, insisted upon by the Indian side, though not denied as valid by the Chinese side, is not the only one; it must be complemented by an inner experience. There must be a 'break-through,' not a mere 'going along.' The older tradition emphasizing the break-through was much closer to the original spirit of Buddhism than the one which merely talked about Buddhism. When we talk about something, it means that we are fairly away from it, not right at the center. The viewpoint of the older tradition is from the center of the matter. Being in the center of the experience makes it possible to guide those who are making an approach to it.

This connection between early Tibetan Buddhism and Chinese Buddhism (which was frowned upon at a much later time) is borne out by certain terms. The term Hoshang seems to have been used with reference to Taoism, while the Hoshang Mahāyāna referred to a Buddhist. The qualification of the Hoshang as Mahāyāna brings out the difference that had become marked between two intellectual trends that at first seemed to have been similar to each other. When new ideas come, we assimilate them and put them into our frame of reference in order to give them meaning. There are two possible ways to do this. One way is to use established terms for these new concepts. Our own concepts will be changed by this because another dimension is added. This is a legitimate way and the Chinese used this method by first translating words by Taoist concepts and later by trying to discover the difference.

This poses the problem of preserving identity. Another approach is not to translate the terms for the new concepts at all. They are introduced as a foreign body. Something is being built, but no one understands what it is all about except the person who formulates the new horizon. Since in this case no assimilation has been achieved, a world of fantasy, approaching occultism, is created. It is a paradox in human nature that, on the one hand, one attempts

*Longsal Nyingpo, an important Nyingma terton who helped to refound Katok Monastery in Kham in 1656*

to break away from narrow confines and, on the other, one is afraid of losing one's identity. This kind of struggle went on when translations were made over the centuries. The accusation that the later or 'new' translations no longer contain the spirit of Buddhism certainly can be upheld on these grounds.

As the early ideas came, they were continued and assimilated into rNyingmapa thought and were subsequently developed and preserved into something of what we call the living spirit. The 'new-comers' were only concerned that a text was 'properly' translated and standardized into something that could always be recognized; something that could always be referred to as having an equivalent in the Sanskrit text, whether this had been adequately understood or not. If we look at rNyingma texts, it is extremely difficult to find mere equivalents. The terms used by them acquire meaning in usage and have to be explained. Reading a rNyingma text is quite different from reading a late dGe-lugs-pa text which is based on the 'new' translation, or even a bKa'-brgyud-pa text which follows very much the 'new' translation.

When we study the works that were translated into Tibetan from Sanskrit, we find that the Sanskrit texts are very much concerned with problems of perception and the Indian predilection for logic. The Indians may be the worst logicians in a practical sense, but they have a tremendous interest in logic and have produced excellent works in this field. But epistemology and logic are not the only perspectives from which to develop a philosophy. A very significant part is taken up by metaphysics. Metaphysics is not so much an attempt to set up a system starting with an initial premise, deducing consequences, and then bringing them together into a coherent picture; metaphysics is a way of looking at things differently. We all see the same world, but it may look differently to each one of us. Since the metaphysician looks at his world in a different way than most of us do, the conclusions he draws from his observations are often in striking contrast to the ones with which we are familiar. This is not because he has started with a set of strange presuppositions from which he derives his peculiar conclusions, but simply because he works out the visions he has had. This is the distinguishing feature of the early rNyingma works. Their authors, above all, had a vision, not merely a conception. This is obvious in the works of Shri Singha which are extremely difficult to understand from a merely conceptual approach. The emphasis is always on the vision—to get rid of all the presuppositions and all the other obstacles that obscure or prevent a clear view.

For political reasons, the rNyingma-pas had to go underground. Only later when the fact was forgotten that there had been any connection of early

*L*o Chen Dharma Shri, the younger brother of Urgyan Ter Dag Lingpa and co-founder of Mindroling Monastery. He and his brother were known as the "Moon and Sun Terma."

90    *Philosophy*

rNyingma-pa thinking with Chinese forms of Buddhism, the rNyingma-pas (as Tibetan Buddhists) could emerge from their hiding where they had preserved their metaphysical interpretation of Buddhism. True, Buddhism had come from India, and, for the recognized forms ('recognized' in the sense that they avoided any reference to or connection with Chinese or other non-Indian forms of Buddhism), it was customary to claim a lineage of transmission from the Indian mahāsiddhas, such as Tilopa, Nāropa, Virūpa and others. The rNyingma-pas were first at a disadvantage. dGa'-rab rdo-rje was too hazy a personage in the consciousness of the people to make him the spiritual patron. But there was one person who had been accepted by all and this person was the 'Precious Guru Padmasambhāva.' His spiritual lineage had been kept alive through the agency of Vairocana, exiled to Kinchwan in Szechuan, and the lineage is the rDzogs-chen-pa order which surpasses all other lines of thought by its profoundity.

This teaching, kept alive since the ninth century, received a new impetus in the eleventh century when 'hidden treasures' (*gter-ma*) were discovered on the basis of a prediction Padmasambhāva is said to have made, and which are believed to have been concealed in caves, statues, and other places by Padmasambhāva himself. Those who discovered these works were subsequently known as *gter-ston* and famous among them are Nyang-ral Nyi-ma 'od-zer (1136–1203), Stag-sham nus-ldan (seventeenth century) and others. When we study these texts (some of them are now available) we can cautiously say that they represent a development of thought following and reflecting the changing conditions over the centuries. When Dudjom Rinpoche, the spiritual head of the rNyingma sect, states that the people live by the *gter-ma*, he has made a most valid statement concerning Tibetan Buddhism because the gter-mas represent the living Buddhism of Tibet. The ideas contained in them are alive and not merely an academic past-time of finding a corresponding Sanskrit term for the Tibetan one.

Although there are many gaps in our knowledge of the 'old' form of Buddhism, we have the works of Shri Singha, and we know the connection that existed with Khotan and Kucha not only in the realm of ideas but also in the field of fine arts. Tibetan art has been deeply influenced both from Khotan and China. Thus Tibet had cultural links with both the East and the West. Important persons in the older traditions such as Vairocana and Vimalamitra who were active in Tibet during the reign of the 'religious kings,' had come from India. Vimalamitra is said to have been 200 years old when he was invited to Tibet and the sources are unanimous in stating that he spent the last years of his life on the Wu Tai Shan in China.

It is significant that Vimalamitra, so prominent among rNyingma-pas, went to China, as it shows the early ties with Chinese Buddhism. Mañjuśri is said to have lived on the Wu Tai Shan which is so sacred to Chinese and Japanese Buddhists, and it is Mañjuśri who urges the youth Sudhana to start on his spiritual quest, as told in the Avatamsaka Sutra. While Manjuśri resides on mount Wu Tai Shan, Samantabhadra does so on mount O-mei in Szechuan where Vairocana lived for some time in exile. It is Samantabhadra who figures most prominently in rNyingmapa thought, not merely as a Bodhisattva like Mañjuśri, but as the very symbol of the Absolute. This is uniquely rNyingmapa. The whole first chapter of kLong-chen rab-'byams-pa's *Chos-dbyings rin-po-che'i mdzod* is devoted to the idea of the absolutely positive in the form of Samantabhadra (*kun-tu bzang-po*).

There is some indication that this idea was present in Chinese Buddhism in its so-called Tantric form, Chen-yen (*mantrayāna*), which was developed into the Shingon doctrine in Japan. There are to my knowledge two passages in this literature which refer to the Buddha Samantabhadra, not the Bodhisattva Samantabhadra, and in this doctrine the term Buddha is used as a symbol for the Absolute which is both existential and cognitive. Unfortunately there is no work in any Western language so far that deals with the philosophical implications of this idea that may well have been a Tibetan contribution to Buddhist thought. We shall have to wait until somebody has the courage or the audacity to tackle this vast problem.

There are many other points that show that a very important development in the history of Buddhism took place and that it is represented by rNyingma philosophy. I would even be so bold as to say that once these points become known we shall have to revise and rewrite the whole history of Buddhist thought. This should not be a matter of regret, but rather another step on the road to knowledge through a better understanding of Buddhism. ✤

# Situational Patterning: Pratityasamutpada

*Becoming's Wheel reveals no known beginning,*
*No maker, no experiencer there.*
*Void with a twelvefold voidness,*
*Nowhere it ever halts*
*Forever it is spinning.*

BHADANTĀCARIYA BUDDHAGHOSA

RESPONSIVENESS, A DYNAMIC and variable function, is an essential characteristic of being human. To be human is always to be in a situation. The experience of one situation after another is one's lived world. We do not use 'world' here in the conventional sense of "that out there over against which I stand" (an abstracting dualism invoking the ghost dance of the Cartesian *res cogitans* and *res extensa*) but rather in the sense of one's realm of lived meaning.

Every situation, then, is in one way nothing but one's experienced narrowness or limit of meanings. This narrowness, which often entails confusion and bewilderment, is for most people the predominant modality of responsiveness. Stated differently, one might say that much of man's experience is marked by a general and seemingly pervasive unsatisfactoriness. This observation constituted the Lord Buddha's first Truth [*duḥkha, sdug-bsngal*].

STEVEN D. GOODMAN is a graduate of the University of California, Berkeley, and has been a student of Tibetan Philosophy and Language for the past four years with Tarthang Tulku, Rinpoche. He teaches Buddhist Philosophy and Psychology at the Nyingma Institute.

Unlike those who hold that miseries are but random happenings in an indifferent universe ("The silence of infinite space frightens me"—Pascal), Lord Buddha observed that there is a regular patterning to this misery (only loosely to be construed as a 'cause' or 'origin'). This observation constituted the Second Truth [*samudaya, kun-'byung*]. Insight into the nature of this pattern of unsatisfactoriness is a central concern in the teaching of the Buddha. Buddhists believe, along with certain enlightened trends of pragmatism, that a person *can* do something about the quality of his life. This 'doing,' however, is not so much just another action among many, but rather the development of a penetrating insight which is appropriate to the situation at hand

This insight [*prajñā, shes-rab*] has a dynamic and incisive quality whose 'tone' is always appreciative. It has nothing to do with the development of a cold, searing *logos* carving out larger and larger chunks of a passive world, which as a prominent feature of post-Industrial society caused Nietzsche to comment, "In every desire to know there is a drop of cruelty." The development of *prajñā* is applied directly to one's experience. It may be focused as an analysis of perceptual and cognitive situations, an analysis which always has a preeminently soteriological function. It is *only* developed for the purpose of cutting through the patterns of habitual unsatisfactoriness. (All attempts to reduce Buddhism to a descriptive psychology or mentalistic philosophy must be likened to saying, for example, that Van Gogh's painting of sunflowers *is* just so many grams of cadmium yellow on a piece of canvas.)

We are presented, then, with the assertion that the best way to do something about the quality of our lives is to develop insight, to analyze those very situations in which we find ourselves. Various techniques have been elaborated in the course of time to help those who earnestly seek a way out of bewilderment and frustration. These methods are always intended as 'pointers,' suggesting the possibility of taking a new look at one's predicament. They were elaborated and developed for the sole purpose of helping one to discern the difference between those modes of being which lead to further entanglement and misery and those which lead to increasing clarity —attunement to reality shorn of all fictive notions and convulsive emotivity.

To the extent that we develop insight, the experienced narrowness of meaning is severed and an attendant feeling of calm insues. The most radical severance gives rise to the broadest expanse of experienced meaning, termed Buddha, *sangs-rgyas*. Buddha does not refer to any person as such, but rather to that dynamic mode of being in which the most intense responsiveness possible is actualized. The possibility of severing one's habitually narrowed experiences was the Lord Buddha's proclamation of the Third Truth [*nirodha, 'gog-pa*].

The careful and systematic expansion of meaningful horizons is what is commonly termed the Path. The demonstration and teaching of this systematic expansion was the proclamation of the Fourth Truth [*mārga, lam*]. These Four Truths constitute the core of the Buddha's message to his fellow men. A thoughtful and serious reflection on the implications of each of the Truths might constitute the decisive step initiating one into the opening and deepening of experience.

### Situational Techniques

There are, of course, many methods and techniques elaborated within the Buddhist tradition. What follows is a detailed presentation of one such technique, best regarded as a sort of "sublime gimmick." 'Sublime' in the sense that to the extent one learns to focus with it, one's horizon of meaning naturally expands. And a 'gimmick' in that the technique itself, and the terms used to describe its application can nowhere be found to exist.

This gimmick emphasizes the predominance of recurring motifs in our experience. Twelve characteristic motifs are emphasized. These twelve items are only 'pointers' highlighting various features of our everyday situations; they can never be isolated, for 'they' are always already imbedded in the field character of our experience.

The method under discussion is termed *pratītyasamutpāda* [*rten-cing-'brel-bar-'byung-ba*]. In terms of its application it might be rendered as "the characteristic features of situational patterning." Its proper use produces heightened awareness about the workings of *karma* [*'phrin-las*] such that habit patterns can be penetrated and broken. By *karma* we indicate the name given to the observation of that intimate relatedness which obtains between one situation and another. It has a two-fold aspect, applying equally to (1) that stream of patterning [*saṃtāna, rgyun*] which we experience as 'ourselves,' and (2) to the entire range of meaningful encounters which we experience as 'our world.'

There is an important attitudinal assumption regulating the potency of this method. As one gains enough insight into his lived situation he comes to realize (or at least strongly suspect) its ever-recurrent unsatisfactoriness. This realization should not be a morbid fixation manifesting as melancholic behavior. It should induce the desire to penetrate more deeply into the causes and conditions of one's life. This desire might be termed a healthy attitude, and should be brought to mind whenever one finds oneself slipping into unhealthy attitudes characterized by: (1) generating unanswerable questions ("what is the meaning of my life," etc.) or (2) fixation on unsatisfactoriness (existential despair, morbidity, etc.).

After a healthy attitude has been established, one should call to mind the Three Marks of Conditioned Existence [*tri-lakṣaṇa, mtshan nyid gsum*] which apply to every aspect of the method. The Three Marks are: (1) Unsatisfactoriness [*duḥkha, sdug bsngal*], meaning the motifs indicated are not inherently desirable. (2) Non-entitativeness [*anātman, bdag-med*], meaning one motif cannot be found to exist in isolation from the other eleven. Each motif is relational in structure and arises in conjunction with the others. (3) Transitoriness [*anitya, mi-rtag-pa*], meaning the cognized existence of these motifs is momentary, consisting of (a) an arising, (b) a fleeting stabilization, and (c) a falling away or break up.

### Twelve Motifs

The term *pratītyasamutpāda* indicates dependence [*pratītya*] upon conditions which are variously originated [*samutpāda*]. It avoids the two interpretative extremes of eternalism and nihilism. Eternalism, in this context, is the false inference that because there is an observed regularity of patterning to our experience, there must be an active agent or 'mover' to that pattern. Nihilism, on the other hand, is the doctrine of those who dispute the claim of there being a regularity of patterning, or that all action is fruitless because it is predetermined by fate.

Our experience is not determined by fate, but by conditions which can be known and changed. The conditional relation is intrinsically causal. That is, there is nothing external to the unfolding situation in which I now find myself. The karmic law of unfoldment is the intrinsic and (to those who look carefully) compulsive patterning of events.

Having briefly characterized the general meaning of the term, we now move to a discussion of each of the twelve motifs.

1. *avidyā, ma-rig-pa.* This is usually rendered as 'ignorance.' It refers to the condition of bewilderment and confusion due to a wrong assessment of reality. As the first of the twelve motifs, it might lend itself to being seen as the 'starting point' or 'cause' of worldly existence. It is not a cosmogenic principle or metaphysical cause, but simply the condition under which our present life develops. Perhaps it is best imagined as a continuous gradient characterizing not so much a particular state of being, but the quality or direction of situational patterning, experienced as a 'falling away from' the modality of 'pristine awareness.' It involves a dimming of clarity and a progressive enmeshing into structures of this-and-that.

2. *saṃskāra, 'du-byed.* This motif refers to the impulse accumulation or energetic activity which always accompanies the direction of situational patterning characterized by the first motif. This activity manifests through the body, speech, and mind as structuralizing forces of our being-in-the-world. It forms the basis of our character, our personal karmic patterning.

3. *vijñāna, rnam-par-shes-pa.* The next motif, *vijñāna*, refers to the partially structured consciousness which follows from the action of *saṃskāra*. It indicates the molding of that energetic activity into a kind of frozen energy, a "partial psychic complex." It is pictured as having a two-fold function. It refers to the cognition of objects which arise in the field character of our

*The Wheel of Life* [bhava-cakra] *represents the cyclic nature of* pratītyasamutpāda,
*shown in the outer circle, beginning in the upper right with the blind man carrying a
stick (ignorance). The six realms of existence are represented in the inner circle,
and the three root defilements (lust, hatred, and ignorance) in the center.*

awareness. It is also seen as a structured stream which is being continually fed from the reservoir of energetic activity. The interplay between *saṃskāra* and *vijñāna* is seen as accounting for all the experiential data associated with the psychological notion of the Unconscious, including memory, dreams, and the eruption of emotive complexes.


4. ***nāma-rūpa, ming-gzugs.*** The *vijñāna* is never found by itself. It has a flashing, grasping quality, jumping from sense objects to objects of imagination quite quickly. It can as easily crystallize and polarize into 'material forms,' called *rūpa*, or into mental functions, called *nāma*.

*Nāma* refers to three components of mental functioning. There is the sensation or tone-awareness of a mental situation. There is also an ideational or labeling function. And finally there is the component of dispositional orientation, the "mood-energy" we bring to a situation.

*Rūpa* refers to the four dynamic structuralizing operations of solidity, cohesion, heat, and motility. They are represented by the elemental symbols of earth, water, fire, and air. The operation of these elemental modes goes to make up what we experience as our physical world, including our body. *Rūpa* embraces the static aspects of embodiment such as cellular, tissue, and organ structures. It also includes the dynamic aspect of body metabolism—electrophysiological pathways, membrane transport, etc.

As a collective term, *nāma-rūpa* indicates the close working of bodily and mental functioning.


5. ***ṣaḍ-āyatana, skye-mched-drug.*** The close working of bodily and mental functioning is further differentiated into the six-fold bases of awareness. These 'bases' [*skye-mched*] are to be pictured as furthering [*mched*] the birth [*skye*] or arising of all sensations which make up our experience. The bases are grouped into internal [*ādhyātmika, nang*] and external [*bāhya, phyi*] supports.

The internal grouping refers to the integration of five sensory capabilities (eye, ear, nose, tongue, body) and a sixth capability which provides the possibility for experiences not connected with one of these five. The sixth is termed non-sensuous or mental, and refers to the capability of all acts of memory, imagination, visualization, etc. These internal bases are not to be confused with the corresponding physical organs, which as such are capable of being anatomically disected. They are simply loci of sensitivity structured such that there arises the experience of 'seeing,' 'hearing,' etc.

The six external bases, which always work in conjunction with the corresponding internal base, refer to the six types of possible 'object' awareness. These bases are the means by which the differentiated aspects, which are fleeting stabilizations in the field character of our awareness, stand out long enough to be appropriated as this-or-that specific object. The external and internal bases should be pictured as working together in pairs. In any given moment there is the two-fold working of a particular modality of awareness (eye-sensitivity and color-forms, ear-sensitivity and sounds, etc.).

6. *sparśa, reg-pa.* The next motif refers to the contact or rapport between the internal and external *āyatana*. This contact gives rise to impressions of tone corresponding to the particular mode of sensing which has been activated.

7. *vedanā, tshor-wa.* This motif points to the six types of tone-awareness, which result from the contact of the *āyatana*. This motif expresses the fact that the experience of seeing, its tone, is quite distinct from hearing, or smelling. Each modality is experientially separable on the basis of (a) the *place* of sensitivity (internal base), (b) the corresponding *structure* of its field (external base), (c) the manner of articulation or relatedness between (a) and (b), termed rapport, and (d) the resulting distinctive tone.

8. *taṇhā, sred-pa.* Following rather automatically and habitually upon the arising of tone-awareness is a corresponding craving or thirst for that which has been experienced. Many types of craving attachment may ensue, depending on (a) which of the six modalities has been activated, and (b) which of the three so-called "motivations" it has been joined to.

The motivation of sensual gratification [*kāma-taṇhā*] is perhaps the most common. It results in simple attachment to whatever arises in one's field of awareness. It is not an overt appropriation, one that we consciously activate. It refers rather to the habitual structuring of experience such that one is compulsively caught up in one situation after another through a process of simple identification and clinging.

One can also be motivated with regards to the desire for 'eternals' [*bhavataṇhā*]. It is the habitual structuring of any sensory impression, any momentary awareness, such that it might be the occasion for securing an eternal realm of peace and contentment.

Finally there is the annihilatory motivation [*vibhavataṇhā*]. It is the automatic structuring of experience such that any sensory activation might be the case of a compulsive thirst to annihilate and destroy. What is commonly regarded as psycho-pathic behavior might be linked particularly with this type of motivation. All three of these possible motivations, it should be remembered, are encompassed within the motif of craving. As such all of them go into structuring the responsiveness of 'normal' human beings.

9. *upādāna, len-pa.* The very nature of craving tends to result in a firm grasping or overt clinging [*upādāna*]. An analogy is commonly used to point up the differences between the motifs of craving and firm grasping: *taṇhā* is that which remains unachieved, like a thief groping for goods in the

dark. *Upādāna*, however, is the fruition of this groping, when the thief finally lays hands on the object of searching.

10. *bhava, srid-pa.* Once the direction of situational patterning has proceeded to the point of overt clinging, a process of becoming, termed *bhava*, is initiated. It refers to the new formation of karmic tendencies. It differs from *saṃskāra* in its temporal reference. *Saṃskāra* refers to tendencies from past situational patternings (lives) which act on the present situation. *Bhava*, however, refers to the creation of new habits and tendencies which will have their fruition in experiences of the future.

11. *jāti, skye-ba.* This motif refers to the fruition of the last motif. It is the first appearance of new patternings, which may be seen in two ways. It refers to being-in-a-new-situation. It also refers to that which finds itself in a new situation. In a psycho-biological model, *jāti* refers to the emergence of a new-born being, appearing, according to the specific history of patterning, in one of six 'life-styles.' These life-styles indicate the general character of experience. They are symbolized by the terms gods, titans, hungry ghosts, animals, denizens of hell, and human. These embrace all the general ways of being-in-a-situation.

12. *jarā-marana, rga-shi.* Once a new situation or a new being has emerged, it is inevitable that the conditions which brought about its appearance will change. This, the last of the twelve motifs, points to the inevitability of decay and death. Decay affects all structures, which are but fleeting stabilizations fed by the energy flow of habitual patterning. When the cessation of the continuity of experience occurs, we speak of death. It is the total breakdown and dissolution of experience and experiencer.

The process of disintegration, destructuring, and entropic scattering yields a nexus of vibratory murkiness which is the condition of *avidyā*, the first motif. Thus the entire structure of patterning feeds back on itself, and is often pictured as a circle of twelve sections, called the Wheel of Life, [*bhava-cakra, srid-pa'i-khor-lo*].

### Applications

There are many possible ways of using this schema. Only a few will be suggested. For example, there are several ways of moving from one motif to another:

> The forward order, from [1] to [2] and so on, through [12], is recommended for those who are deluded about the conditions or origin of the manifold factors of experience. Careful attention to the "logic" of forward movement should, with practice, yield a clearer understanding.

The reverse order of movement is recommended for those who have as their specific concern or confusion the problem of birth, decay and death. Starting from a contemplation of these motifs, one would then move backwards through clinging, thirst, tone-awareness, contact, etc., gradually penetrating the connectedness and 'origin' of each motif.

One can also start from the middle [8] and proceed in reverse order up to [1]. This is meant as an exercise for penetrating into situations of past patterning so as to account for the present.

Starting from the middle [8] and proceeding to the last term [12] is for the purpose of penetrating into present conditions such that one might better understand the probable consequences in the future.

For those whose psychical make-up is dominated by speculative confusions [*diṭṭhicaritas*], contemplation of motifs [1] through [7] is sufficient; showing the unbroken continuity of causes and conditions.

For those dominated by attractions towards worldly things [*taṇhācaritas*], contemplation of motifs [8] through [12] is recommended. It counteracts the belief in permanence [*sassata-diṭṭhi*] by showing the inevitability of decay and death.

These motifs may be regarded as occuring simultaneously or in temporal succession. In the latter case the motifs [1] and [2] represent the past, number [3] through [10] the present, and [11] and [12] the future.

As mentioned before, the entire schema is a representation of the direction of patterning, which, as the predominant modality of responsiveness, is marked by suffering, frustration and unhappiness. These motifs are compulsively linked together, but are capable of being broken.

Of these twelve motifs, *avidyā* [1], *taṇhā* [8], and *upādāna* [9] represent the predominance of bewildering emotivity [*kleśa*]. *Saṃskāra* and *bhava* represent the predominance of consequent action patterning [*karma*]. The seven remaining motifs provide the continuing ground of unsatisfactoriness [*duḥkha*]. Emotivity, compulsive actions, and unsatisfactoriness are often pictured as the three 'legs' of the tripod called *saṃsāra*. The removal, through penetrating insight [*prajñā*], of any one of these legs is sufficient to topple the entire structure.

This method, and the techniques of application briefly indicated above, are only meant as suggestions. As an analysis of the 'causes' of unsatisfactoriness, it is vulnerable to being wrongly assessed as a mere conceptual schema. Like all methods of the Buddha's teaching, it was elaborated to help one gain a new perspective. As such, it demands serious use. Otherwise it is nothing but an intellectual plaything, to be fitted into our already burgeoning files of 'interesting data.' ❄

# Kun-gzhi:
# The Positiveness of Being

*Mind, intellect, and the formed contents*
*of that mind are Being-Itself,*
*So too are the world and all that seems*
*from It to differ,*
*All things that can be sensed and the perceiver,*
*Also dullness, aversion, desire, and enlightenment.*

SARAHA

Simply stated, a major insight inherent in the Mahāyāna is the primacy of 'mind,' and the phenomenal presence of the actual world came to be a presence before a 'mind.' The world exists, not only as an object perceived by the individual [*pudgala*], but also as something being created by each individual in his subjectivity. Of the five composite aggregates [*skandha*] which constitute the individual as impermanent [*anitya*] and without an abiding principle [*anātman*], the one that performs this discriminative function is the consciousness aggregate [*vijñāna*]. Through the dynamic instrumentality of consciousness, man's thinking processes were looked upon as fluctuating around an orientational center, which was called 'mind.' It was the mentalistic Vijñānavāda school which took this capacity, a sort of 'mind-sense,' and extended it into a coherent theory which attempted to describe the

LAWRENCE GRUBER holds a degree in Religious Studies and Psychology from California State University, Fullerton. He is a student of Tarthang Tulku and studies at the Nyingma Institute.

$\mathcal{N}$*agarjuna*
*the great Indian*
*Mahasiddha who*
*founded the logic*
*of the Middle*
*Way and brought*
*the Prajnaparamita*
*from the Nagas.*

nature of 'mind' in such a manner that the entire scope of an individual's perceptual configuration took on the nature of a unitary process. It was a direct refutation of the independent existence of anything apart from the mere fictional constructions [*parikalpa*] present in our thinking, which only clouds the sense of the real. A major criticism of this formal tendency, however, was that it created an interpretation of 'mind' that was dangerously subjectivistic in nature.

When these ideas were transplanted to Tibet, the status of 'mind' became less positional (viz., a tendency away from pan-subjectivism) and more non-positional. In psychological terms, this grew to the point where each 'state of mind' was no less favored than 'mind' itself and where every state carried with it a sort of ultimately positive respectability, whether it be filled with a negative or positive feeling content. In this way, 'mind' was thought of as a singular substratum, an extensive continuum, which represents an ever-widening ground that becomes more all-inclusive as man's preconceived self-image becomes less rigid in his preoccupation with deadening projects. The shift is from a positional consciousness in terms of a subject-object dichotomy [*vikalpa*] to a non-positional consciousness which is still conscious

*A*ryadeva,
*born from a*
*lotus, he became*
*Nagarjuna's closest*
*disciple and*
*expanded the*
*application of the*
*Madhyamika dialectic.*

of something and where that something is not a 'self.' The normal status of mind is that it is conscious of some 'thing' out there, involving a uniquely configured perceptual process of such-and-such a nature.

As it is the task of Buddhism to lead man out of this subject-object division which only makes us divided against ourselves, the Nyingmapas, in their development of the Atiyoga [*rDzogs-chen*] tradition, extended the description of the noetic capacity of mind far beyond any other previous school of Buddhism.* Atiyoga developed from the teachings of the great Adi-Buddha Samantabhadra (being a symbol for Dharmakāya or Absolute Being) who promulgated the highest teachings of the Tantras.**

In order for the all-positiveness and all-inclusiveness of the final goal

---

* The trend was in the direction of an ontological framework rather than simply more epistemology (viz., the study of perceptual processes) with which Indian Buddhist scholars were so historically preoccupied. In the context of Buddhist philosophy, ontology is always the study of Being, as opposed to the study of some particular being.

** For a fuller explanation of Tantra, see Herbert V. Guenther, *Buddhist Philosophy in Theory and Practice* (Penguin, 1972), Chapter 6.

(enlightenment) to be something attainable by sentient beings, something very essential and very precious must be present in our consciousness. This 'something' must be present in the samsaric mind as well as the nirvanic mind; for such a final goal to be possible, we need 'somewhere' to start from. Here, Saṃsāra and Nirvāṇa cannot be thought of as separate entities, but simply ways in which a person chooses to view [dṛṣṭi] his world. This all-ground, which is nothing in itself, is the foundation for what we interpret as Saṃsāra (a more or less frustrating way of being), and Nirvāṇa (Being-in-itself). This all-ground is termed kun-gzhi, and its development by the Nyingmapas in both theory and practice is an exceedingly complex one.

As human beings, we can examine our experiences and act upon our understanding to produce a more unified conception of ourselves. We can be constantly engaged in petty concerns or we can choose to develop that noetic capacity which brings about conditions appropriate to enlightenment. This process is immediately accessible to us and occurs at every level of our development, even though clouded thoughts may hinder us from attaining this vision for even a short while.

Kun-gzhi has an entirely homogeneous nature. We may say "It was but a dream" after we have unsuccessfully attempted to grasp such an experience. Kun-gzhi leads us to that perspective inasmuch as it 'feels' like a 'movement' out of something and into something entirely different and yet greatly appreciated. In order for something to be an existentially leading principle, it must rest on two related poles, the origin and the goal—the former being beginningless Saṃsāra and the latter being absolute Buddhahood. This statement, of course, is misleadingly simple. 'Saṃsāra' may be literally translated as 'moving about in circles.' As we observe ourselves in such a condition, we can learn to move about in less narrow circles through medi-tation. The actualization of kun-gzhi thus allows us to see more clearly where we are and where we are going in each new situation. We move from one situation to another, each with its own unique set of emotionally toned dispositions. With insight into the nature of our internal experience, we can begin to draw a sort of cognitive map towards enlightenment. We are the embodiment of the possibility of achieving the final goal right here and now. In order to achieve this, we must begin to differentiate our experiences without creating further confusion.

The beginning phase of kun-gzhi is something like confusion, or our ordinary (unenlightened) way of relating to the world of appearance. How-ever, as we gradually learn to witness the action patterns of our thoughts and feelings, we can discover how we fall prey to the artificial nature of our interpretative thoughts, or feelings highly charged with emotivity. We know inherently that bliss supreme cannot come out of such thoughts and emo-tional states—unexamined fears and disruptive dissatisfactions—so we must progressively 'awaken' into the 'all-ground,' kun-gzhi. This awakening of attention to thoughts and feelings—how we create our world—surpasses the limiting concept that all thoughts are inalterably determined by fixed situations and that we have no control over the karmic development of our own lives.

In order to understand more about *kun-gzhi*, we must first think of ourselves as a synthesis of body and mind which forms a continuum. If we examine ourselves as a complex [*skandha*] of thoughts, feelings, expectations, and physical sensations, we can find in ourselves an orientational center from which we may reflectively observe a continuous, indeterminate substratum. This fluctuating, momentary awareness is our initial conception of ourselves —the sort of thing a psychologist looks for when he administers personality inventories. These individual patterns of the mind comprehending itself reflect certain residues or conditioned habits which carry with them a more substantive character. Here we are going backwards, away from the neutral *kun-gzhi* and toward the very essence of the samsaric mind. We are now (and possibly for once) stepping out of ourselves and looking backwards at ourselves—at those particular traits and dispositions bound up within us which somehow conveniently assure us 'we know who we are.'

While we may examine 'how we are' generally, it is especially important to maintain awareness of ourselves during those deeper emotive bursts of especially high intensity which carry with them certain disturbances which eventually resettle like dust into how we are generally. Both conditions are impermanent: the first compounded into changing fragments or moods, and the second devoid of any insightful continuity. Like a static charge, these particular traces and dispositions are held together in a manner that is so firm that the 'intrinsic perception' of the enlightenment-mind [*dharmajñānakāya*] cannot penetrate the seemingly preferential insensitivity to our own functioning and conditioning. Consequently, an artificial world (our apparent 'situational context') is created which is filled with distortions—much like our perception of a visual field when the light is dimmed and many shadows move indistinctly.

*Kun-gzhi* itself, however, cannot be talked about directly, for words do not suffice. When discussing matters of man's Being, we can explicate but not explain. As an experientially initiated possibility, *kun-gzhi* takes man out of his narrowness and impresses upon him the actualization and appreciation of what we may call a 'freeing motion.' *Kun-gzhi*, in general, is the movement away from the superficial boundaries of our own way of looking at ourselves, towards an intrinsically open situation. This situation continues to persist through the embodiment of our five senses and the responsive consciousness, which act in harmony to what is seen as a changing world. Meanwhile, the changing world of appearance is recognized as just that: reality persists as its very own being, irrespective of any conceptions we may have about it.

Through the insight of *kun-gzhi*, everything worth knowing becomes knowable because everything is seen as totally pure and devoid of the obscuring qualities which create a mind lost in dichotomies. This 'freeing motion' is a gradual awakening into an intrinsic perception which is felt as being somehow present, while at the same time left uncategorized. By not being understood as some 'particular,' this meditation becomes the sharpest possible value-oriented mode of perceiving, and as such leads one out of the dizzying labyrinths of novel experiencing. As the freeing motion is felt, all appearances that come by way of the six senses freely arise and carry with them multifaceted reflections. As the perceptual processes harmonize, they are acted upon with a kind of playfulness that is co-terminous with the understanding that whatever is apprehended is seen as having an apparitional nature. What is experienced arises from nothing ("it was only a dream") and returns to nothing and thus cannot be concretized into a thing. The distinction here is between 'intrinsic perception' and normal 'categorical perception.' With the latter we can only live in 'our' world of habit-forming thoughts which fetter our mind with the unreality of a subject apprehending some object external to our consciousness; whereas 'intrinsic perception' leads us subtly and spontaneously out of our logical fictions and into an appreciative understanding [*prajñā*] of the absolute positiveness of Being, *kun-gzhi*.

This ultimate positiveness sees the relative dualistic conception of

*D*ignaga, founded and systematized the study of Buddhist logic.

Saṃsāra and Nirvāṇa as one. Thus, *kun-gzhi* is the neutral all-ground because in its positiveness it appreciates the self-sameness of Being (as opposed to some being). This self-sameness of Being is synonymous with the understanding that all things are devoid of an ultimate principle. Such an intrinsic perception allows the individual to have a vision of the creative spontaneity of a situation without dividing thoughts into some emotionally charged past, uncomfortable present, or anticipated future. *Kun-gzhi*, as a revealing vision and a self-renewing presence, considers each moment of 'mind' as having within itself the fullest measure of concept-less spontaneity and 'pristine awareness' imaginable. ❧

PART FOUR

# PRACTICE

# *Mantra*

Mantras have been used for thousands of years by yogic practitioners as a method for cutting through negativity and obscurations, as well as creating balance in the body and mind. If used properly, these mantras can help to open the heart center. Each of them corresponds with a particular energy potential or aspect of mind and is related to one of the manifestations of the Buddha. Many benefits can come both for oneself and for other beings through the sincere practice of chanting these mantras.

## TATYĀTA ŌM MUNI MUNI MAHĀ MUNI
## SHĀKYAMŪNIYE SŌHA

The mantra of Shakyamuni Buddha helps to counteract delusion
and aid in self-healing.

## ŌM MAṆI PADME HŪM HRĪ

This mantra cures negative emotions and suffering through the limitless
compassion of Avalokiteshvara.

# ŌṀ ĀH HŪṀ VAJRA GURU PADMA SIDDHĪ HŪṀ

Guru Padma Sambhava's mantra is the antidote for confusion and
frustration in this Dark Age.

# ŌṀ ĀH RA PA TSA ṆA DHĪ

Manjushri's mantra develops Wisdom, symbolized by the two-edged
flaming sword which cuts through ignorance.

# ŌṀ VAJRA PĀṆI HŪM PHĀT

The mantra of Vajrapani creates strength to overcome self-destruction,
fear, and emotional problems.

# ŌṀ TĀRE TUTTĀRE TURE SŌHA

Through praying the mantra of Tara, the Mother of Compassion,
all beings may receive protection.

# ŌṀ VAJRASATTVA HŪṀ

All defilements and obscurations can be purified through
the mantra of Vajrasattva. ❖

# Studying the Dharma

*Since in this evil age the life of man does not last long*
*and since it is impossible to reach the limits of what can*
*be known, you should strive to attend to that which*
*is essential rather than dabbling in too many things.*

YE-SHES RGYAL-MTSHAN

Buddhism has many different techniques or practices which apply to different situations and our different levels of consciousness. Some teachings stress self-help through disciplined inquiry and self-control. Others emphasize compassion and understanding. But just as you cannot talk to a breadmaker about the intricacies of sending a rocket to the moon, nothing can be understood properly or deeply without an initial experience of the teachings and a certain amount of practice and skill. Vajrayana has always been taught and understood as a path for the very strong, and this path involves complete openness to each experience.

On one hand, we live in a very scientific, technological society. Modern people are not too interested in religions that stress dogmatic ideas and require rigid conformity. Yet each individual has some basic need for spiritual fulfillment, some deeper, internal source of meaning in life. These teachings investigate everything about life and the world: how we perceive, how we feel, how we judge and think. Everything depends on our direct experience of the teachings in daily life. This is our freedom: through deep meditation and exploration of the mind, awareness develops spontaneously within each situation.

We search and search, but who is investigating? What is this individual experience of meditation? How do we look into the thought? Trying to find the 'I' in our daily experience cuts the root of habitual concepts and reactions.

Vajrayana looks behind the ideas, conceptions, and pleasures, and uses each situation for growth. As imagined limitations and useless clingings slowly loosen, our energies become liberated from time-consuming confusions and unclear assumptions. By letting go of self-grasping concepts, awareness becomes positive, open and balanced. Vajrayana can thus be very important to modern society.

In America, many different kinds of experience are possible. But this can be dangerous for someone who is just trying to satisfy his needs for pleasure. Human nature exists in Samsara, and what we feel is most desirable can often be just another trap. The attitude of 'experimentation' that is so popular here can be very useful. But we must first of all understand that the material with which we are working, the data we are collecting, is really our own mind.

In Vajrayana we follow the tradition of the lineage of teachers who have passed on their wisdom and skillful means from Guru to disciple since the time of the Buddha. To know the roots of one's teaching is very important. Otherwise, like all foundations, whatever we erect will collapse.

Buddha's teachings were specifically designed for man's consciousness. Thus this tradition, as passed on from teacher to student, is very rare and precious—we say *jewel-like*—because it has proved effective in cutting through the intricacies and subtleties of samsaric mind. But in modern society, no real tradition exists between teachers and students. The relationship is more external, like a business contract. In order for the teachings really to take root and become fruitful, an atmosphere of mutual trust and confidence must be developed between the teacher and disciple. Openness and freedom from preconceptions is the key to establishing this relationship. Perseverance in practice and faith in the effectiveness of the Buddha and Dharma are the means to maintain it.

In Vajrayana, one's Guru is held to be even more important than the Buddha, for he is the one who initiates the student into the teachings. Without a Guru, one cannot tread the path of Vajrayana. And without deep respect and devotion to the Guru, one cannot receive the blessings and power which flow from the Buddha through the Guru's lineage to the student.

It is said that how we study the Dharma is actually more important than what we study. The Tibetans liken the student who comes to the Guru only to gain benefits for himself to the musk hunter, who kills the musk deer only for his precious scent, caring nothing for the life of the deer.

To be able to receive teachings of the Dharma has traditionally been considered a rare and useful opportunity. Milarepa's songs reflect his gratitude and devotion to Marpa for graciously bestowing the gift of his teachings. Throughout the lineage of Buddhist teachers there has been a mutual responsibility between the teacher and disciple to persevere in the practice of the Dharma until full understanding and compassion are born. Without this dedication to the teacher, path, and goal, success in the Dharma cannot be found.

Studying the Dharma is very different from studying at the University. If success is to be achieved, we must allow the teachings to touch all aspects of our lives. As our understanding deepens we will find that we are becoming in many senses a wholly new person.

But all this basically depends on our willingness to study seriously. The Dharma is no game; we can gain nothing if we only play at it. But as much as we are able to give of ourselves to the Guru and to our practices, deep, positive feelings will result in our lives. Discouragement may arise if we feel we do not receive results quickly enough. But perseverance and patience can counteract these obstacles, and faith can renew one's efforts until success is gained.

In the beginning we may just skim the teachings and become excited about having discovered something—but not really understand. Buddha's teachings come from direct experience with life. So we need to look deeply at our own lives, remember our past experiences, and examine the pervasive nature of impermanence. Our problems are mostly self-created, while mind runs here and there like a monkey trapped in a house. This anxiety situation, our dissatisfaction, can give us the energy to change, to transmute negative mental attitudes. We can thus learn to use each situation—just as it is. This keeps the meditation experience alive. We can stay in that understanding and awareness no matter where we are. ❖

# Activities at the Center

*As lightning is seen brightly for an instant*
*in the darkness of a clouded night, so perhaps, for once,*
*the thought of the world may be turned, by the gesture*
*of the Buddha, to good things for an instant.*

ŚĀNTIDEVA

THE TIBETAN NYINGMA MEDITATION CENTER has grown considerably in the past year and a half and has been blessed with many visitors, new students, and professionals who have taken a deep interest in the spread of the Dharma and Tibetan Buddhism in the West. In the winter of 1972, His Holiness Dudjom Rinpoche, the head of the Nyingma school, visited Berkeley as part of a world tour. Since forced to leave Tibet in 1959, His Holiness has been living in India with his family where he continues to teach and head the oldest of the Tibetan Buddhist schools. While at the Center, Dudjom Rinpoche held a number of special ceremonies and initiations, gave personal interviews and meditation instruction, and answered the questions of the many students and visitors he met. His presence was a great source of inspiration, for Dudjom Rinpoche is one of the most respected Buddhist teachers living today. His wife and three children accompanied him. His visit also coincided with the opening of the second Sacred Art of Tibet exhibit in San Francisco and he blessed the exhibit in an elaborate ceremony opening night.

The Sacred Art exhibit, held throughout December at Lone Mountain College, was an impressive successor to the first Tibetan art exhibit held in 1971. This was perhaps the most extensive collection of Tibetan art shown in

*His Holiness
Dudjom Rinpoche,
the head of the
Nyingma School.*

the West, and guides gave many people a greater understanding of the complex and beautiful symbolism of Tibetan art.

The Sacred Art of Tibet exhibit is being presented even more extensively in 1974. Throughout the month of March, the exhibit was held at the Berkeley Arts and Crafts Center and featured many rare tankas and rupas. From June 21 to July 18, a major showing of Tibetan art will be presented at Grace Cathedral in San Francisco. This exhibit will contain the largest collection of Tibetan tankas and rupas ever presented by the Center, together with lectures, films, and other special events. This collection will then tour some of the major cities of the United States throughout the summer. More Westerners will thus have an opportunity to view this Tibetan sacred art than ever before.

Lama Gyatul Domang was the first of several lamas to live at TNMC. He soon became a favorite at the Center and was greatly respected for his gentleness and wit. Unfortunately, he had to return to Canada in early 1973. During his stay however, he helped arrange the initiations during Dudjom Rinpoche's visit and took part in the yearly *Long-chen-pa Sadhana* held in February 1973.

This Sadhana celebrates the Parinirvana of Long-chen-pa (Kun-mKyen kLong-chen Rab-'Jam-pa, 1308–1363), who is widely recognized as the greatest lama and scholar of the Tibetan lineage who, as a Dharmakaya manifestation, articulates the absolute and unsurpassable understanding of Reality. He systematized and taught both the oral-transmission of Padma Sambhava and the writings of the Indian pandit, Vimalamitra, on Ati-yoga, the practice which leads directly to the attainments of complete and perfect Buddhahood.

Long-chen-pa Sadhana is traditionally celebrated in Tibet by lamas only, and normally lasts a week. Here, however, a simpler sadhana is performed which lasts five days. During this ceremony, many pujas, or offering mandalas, are performed, together with the continuous chanting of the Vajra Guru mantra. The serious effort and concentration such a ceremony requires has a powerful effect on the mind. The proper performance of sadhana is in itself the full practice of the Six Perfections and presents students with a special opportunity to overcome difficulties created by rigid habit patterns. The ceremonies held at the Center generally include textual recitation, mantra chanting, visualization, and meditation. Using these practices, one's body, speech, and mind are offered to all the Buddhas, with one's accumulated merit offered to all sentient beings.

In the spring of 1973, an effort was made to bring more lamas here to teach and translate. Lama Golok Jigtse, a Nyingma monk from the same area of Tibet as Tarthang Tulku, spent several months at the Center, and Lama Do Drup Chen Rinpoche, head of the Namgyal Institute of Tibetology in Sikkim, spent the summer here. However, they had to leave in early fall to meet commitments elsewhere.

Lamas Do Drup Chen and Golok Jigtse were present for the *Nyung Nay Sadhana* which was held at the Center in June. This ceremony, lasting for three days, is representative of the Hinayana and Mahayana branches of Buddhist development, as the Long-chen-pa Sadhana is of the Vajrayana. Nyung Nay is a time of intense practice and purification, and includes a 48-hour period when students take the traditional vows of a monastic community, fast, and observe silence. There is much merit from the pure observance of vows, and this ceremony emphasizes compassion for all beings. Nyung Nay also coincides with the Center's annual observance of Shakyamuni Buddha's birth and Parinirvana.

After two months of reconstruction—painting, refinishing and decorating—the Nyingma Institute opened in June 1973 with an eight-week Human Development Training Program offered by Tarthang Tulku. The response was very encouraging, for over sixty psychologists and mental health professionals came to the Institute to spend the summer learning the basic psychological approach and practical therapeutic techniques of Tibetan Buddhism. The Training Program ended with an official open house which was held at the new Institute building near the Berkeley campus. Several hundred people came to enjoy the small exhibit of Tibetan art, films, Eastern dances, and outdoor buffet. The heads of the San Francisco Zen Center and other California Buddhist congregations were also present. Regular quarterly classes in Buddhist theory and practice began at the Institute in October.

This February, the Center celebrated the fifth annual Long-chen-pa Sadhana, taking off a few days from work to meditate and practice. Early in June we will be observing the fourth Nyung Nay Sadhana dedicated to Avalokiteshvara, and celebrating the enlightenment of Shakyamuni Buddha.

These ceremonies are open to those whom Rinpoche accepts as practicing students. This implies a deep commitment to personal growth and study with Rinpoche, practice of the Teachings, and the traditional performance of the *Bum Nga*. The *Bum Nga* is a series of five different practices involving prostrations, prayers, mantras, visualization, and meditation. These practices develop the Six Perfections, beginning with initial openness and generosity, and are essential to initiation into the higher Vajrayana practice. Their effect continues in daily life, as the meditation experience and growth in awareness permeates every situation and activity.

'Practice' means to incorporate, to directly experience the teachings for oneself, practically and effectively. Theoretical knowledge, while useful and necessary, is like the moon in water: whatever is researched and reflected upon surely points the way. The depth and totality of Nyingma teachings integrate formal understanding with the experience of each moment. As the mind becomes more lucid, tranquil, and free, compassion deepens and wisdom grows. ❖

# The Nyingma Institute

*In so far as in this evil age, sentient beings,*
*engulfed in utter darkness, often take to wrong ways,*
*they must first find certainty about the unerring way*
*by examining critically and with subtle logic*
*the meaning of the Buddha's words.*

YE-SHES RGYAL-MTSHAN

THE OPENING OF the Nyingma Institute in 1973 created a totally new channel for transmitting to Americans the Vajrayana teachings.

The purpose of the Nyingma Institute is to become a major center for Western students, scholars and laymen to preserve and practice the psychological and philosophical concepts of Tibetan Buddhism. Under the guidance of Tarthang Tulku, Rinpoche, the Nyingma Institute offers an accredited program in Tibetan Buddhism and Studies of Consciousness. A variety of courses combines the intellectual with the experiential and emphasizes personal growth in awareness. Buddhism's psychology is the result of more than two thousand years of subtle observation and application. Thus, the teachings of Buddha, and the practical insight that follows, are meant to develop man's conscious awareness.

While similar to a Western institution in form and scope, the Institute wishes to remain close to its founding philosophy. Tibetan Buddhism is not a set of facts to be learned or theories to be memorized, but is basically and primarily a method of reaching a more meaningful kind of life, and communicating it to others. Therefore the major emphasis is on teaching courses that give increased depth and practical understanding to people's lives.

The Tibetan Nyingma Meditation Center was first formed to provide a Western center of study. The Center served a central core of about a hundred immediate students of the lama and also offered to the public monthly weekend seminars on various aspects of Tibetan Buddhism. So far, over 1000 people have come searching for a deeper understanding of the philosophy, psychology, art and history of Tibet, as well as for basic instruction in meditation. For the last year, these seminars have been held at the Nyingma Institute.

The Institute opened last summer with an intensive eight-week training program offered by Lama Tarthang Tulku for professionals in the mental health fields. It was successful beyond expectations and drew 25 Ph.D.'s, psychotherapists, clergymen, lawyers and others, as well as 18 graduate students from 20 states and 2 foreign countries. Here they explored their minds by considering aspects of Nyingma philosophy and psychology, and by practicing Nyingma meditation techniques and physical exercises.

A wide range of courses—the psychological understanding and therapeutic body-mind techniques of the Nyingma tradition—have been offered to over 400 people in the first three quarters, while an initial class of twelve graduate students has been accepted into the Master's program. In addition, a number of students from nearby campuses have arranged to take courses at the Institute for credit.

When Buddhism appeared in Tibet, a tremendous effort was made to carefully preserve and establish all the philosophy, psychology, and practices that make up the Dharma. In a relatively short time, Tibetans completely established the three schools of Hinayana, Mahayana and Vajrayana. A lama would spend a third of his life studying with various teachers to gain a comprehensive and practical experience of the Dharma. This effort was successful in preserving thousands of volumes of Indian Buddhism in careful translation.

In the beginning, the greatest scholars were invited to come from India to teach in Tibetan monasteries. And Tibetan scholars and translators (*lotsawas*) would also travel to India. These translators were interested in the living value of what these texts contained. They would study and meditate for years to fully assimilate the total meaning of this experience before trying to produce a Tibetan text from the Sanskrit original. Translators would normally produce only a few complete texts in their whole lifetime. While the Tibetans worked to preserve the Buddhist tradition which was dying out in India, they also added their own insights based upon experiences from their own culture and traditions.

This tradition continued in relative isolation for many centuries while the rest of the world went on in other ways. Tibet did not have to face the impact of modern culture until just recently, and then in the unsympathetic form of war. The invasion and occupation of Tibet virtually obliterated this unique civilization. Nearly all the temples were destroyed, ancient libraries were burned, and tens of thousands of lamas were reported to have been either killed or driven out of monastic life and forbidden to teach. In America the situation would be analogous to the total destruction of all colleges, universities and great libraries throughout the country.

A small number of lamas escaped the 1959 holocaust and now live as refugees in India and other states bordering Tibet. These refugees are of special concern and interest, for they are the sole repositories of a particularly valuable tradition. Lamas fleeing to India were concerned with preserving this heritage above all else, and thus each school of Tibetan Buddhism was able to save some of the ancient texts. Many of these texts are written in symbolic or allegorical language, or use words whose meanings require direct experience. Their systematic explorations search the outer reaches of human consciousness—an investigation which is as yet little understood in the West.

When Tarthang Tulku came in 1969 there were few Tibetan lamas in America teaching their traditions. In spite of the initial lack of material assistance, it now seems possible that the Tibetan heritage can be saved. For

*T*arthang Tulku, Rinpoche, and Dr. Herbert V. Guenther

through the shared interest and enthusiasm of Tibetans and those who have come in contact with them, each year a growing number of Westerners are beginning to learn these direct experiential techniques.

### Masters Degree Program

The Institute offers a masters degree in Nyingma Training and Studies of Consciousness. The Tibetan concept of "mastery" is different from merely having acquired a masters degree. The goal of the Institute is that the graduate of this program will skillfully use this knowledge and communicate it to others.

Nyingma teachings bring the theory of philosophy and the practice of psychology together. Training at the Institute includes three major interest areas: *Studies of Consciousness, Philosophy,* and *Cultural Studies,* including the art, language, and history of Tibet, as well as Nyingma psycho-physiological exercises.

The courses listed below are currently being offered for credit at the Institute during the year 1973–74. Many of these courses are also offered as weekend seminars. For further information, contact the Nyingma Institute 1815 Highland Place, Berkeley, California, 94709.

| STUDIES OF CONSCIOUSNESS | PHILOSOPHY | CULTURAL STUDIES |
|---|---|---|
| Nyingma Meditation I, II | Buddhist Philosophy | Tibetan Language I, II, III |
| Contemplation Exercises | Buddhist Phil. Systems | Sanskrit |
| Buddhist Psychology | Consciousness Readings | Kum Nye Relaxation I, II |
| Psychology of Meditation | Nyingma Philosophy I, II | Tanka Theory & Practice |
| Nyingma Teaching Methods | Mahayana Buddhism | Intro. Tibetan Buddhism |
| Meditation and Retreat | Buddhism in Tibet | Tibetan History |
| | Madhyamika Thought | |

In addition to Tarthang Tulku, the Institute faculty includes eighteen Buddhist scholars, professional psychologists, and advanced students of the Center. Several of those psychologists involved in the 1973 Human Development Training Program have begun teaching certain Nyingma techniques of self-analysis and relaxation at the Institute and elsewhere.

During the fall quarter Dr. D. R. Ruegg, noted Buddhist scholar of the University of Washington, presented a seminar in the *Madhyamika* dialectic. Dr. Herbert V. Guenther, well-known scholar, translator, and author from the University of Saskatchewan taught a seminar and several classes in Tibetan Buddhist philosophy, psychology, and history.

### Human Development Training Program

Tarthang Tulku will again teach an eight-week full-time program in the summer of 1974. The Training Program is basically designed for psychologists, mental health practitioners, and graduate students who can expect to learn techniques which are of use in their work. While the basic philosophy and theory behind the practices will be covered, it is essentially not a reading course. The Training Program is primarily experiential and should take the full time of the participant to be beneficial, including eight hours a day of meetings, and individual practices in the evenings and on weekends. The course includes an introduction to meditation, Kum Nye relaxation, Buddhist and Vajrayana philosophy and psychology, and emphasizes practices which are useful in therapy. [July 8 to August 30, 1974]

## Buddhist Philosophy Training Program

This is an intensive five-week training seminar in intermediate and advanced Buddhist philosophy, with emphasis on Tibetan contributions. This seminar is designed for philosophy teachers—especially teachers of Asian philosophy—and others who are interested in deepening their understanding of Buddhist philosophy.

A distinguished group of scholars will trace the development of Mahayana and Vajrayana thought, and offer comparative views to provide an in-depth orientation to Buddhist theory and practice. Instructors include, L. S. Kawamura (Univ. of Saskatchewan), Lewis Lancaster (Univ. of California, Berkeley), Yuichi Kajiyama (Kyoto University), Huston Smith (Syracuse University), and Tarthang Tulku. [June 17 to July 19, 1974] ✤

# Nyingma Country Center

*When the Iron Bird flies and horses run on wheels,*
*the Tibetan people will be scattered like ants*
*across the world, and the Dharma will come*
*to the land of the Red Man.*

PADMA SAMBHAVA

To REALLY TEACH and preserve Vajrayana Buddhism, a quiet, somewhat isolated area is needed where a practical, living Tibetan-American community can take root and grow. Long before Tarthang Tulku's arrival— when his teachers stressed the importance of passing on this lineage to the West—Rinpoche's long-term view has been to develop a rural community in America. Anyone who wishes might thus have access to the full teachings of the Vajrayana and an environment in which to practice them.

So far, the Tibetan Nyingma Meditation Center, Dharma Press, and the Nyingma Institute have almost magically evolved to develop a core of practicing students, an established publishing and printing company, and an academic community devoted to Buddhist Studies and the integration of Western and Eastern psychology.

Now it is important to continue, for we wish to develop an entire community of Americans and Tibetans which is completely self-sufficient. Specifically we plan:

- To involve Western scientists, scholars, psychologists and Orientalists in the development of a central academic university
- To work on translations of significant Tibetan meditation texts
- To train artists capable of preserving the Tibetan tanka tradition

- To develop a retreat center for friends, benefactors, and those interested in practicing the teachings
- To establish a retirement community of older people, facilities for teaching the young, and appropriate medical facilities for ourselves and the neighboring community
- To develop a farming community, with gardens and livestock, which is self-sufficient; and, most important,
- To bring Tibetan lamas, scholars, artists, translators, craftsmen and their families to transmit the direct lineage of the Nyingma tradition in America.

In addition, this land will provide sufficient space for the traditional 3-year retreat of higher religious practices for which Rinpoche has been training his students.

So far, many have donated time, services, and money, and we graciously thank our friends and benefactors. The Nyingma tradition can survive in the West with your continuing help. This project is an investment for the rest of our lives, and for the success of the Dharma in America. ✤

# Tibetans in India

*Both directly and indirectly one must act only*
*for the welfare of sentient beings. One should bend*
*everything to their welfare and their Enlightenment.*

ŚĀNTIDEVA

THOSE RELATIVELY FEW Tibetan lamas and scholars who escaped from
Tibet after its invasion hold the future of the Tibetan practices and traditions.
While a few of these men have gone on to study and teach in universities
throughout the world, most of them live in destitute conditions. A number of
excellent Tibetan scholars studying in India and neighboring Himalayan
countries have a real comprehension of the meaning of their religious and
psychological texts. But so far little has been done to transmit the tantric
practices of the Vajrayana to the modern world, and only lately have the useful
psychological and therapeutic techniques become known to the psychological
establishment.

The Tibetan Nyingma Meditation Center has always aimed at expanding beyond the single person of Tarthang Tulku to include many
teaching and translating lamas. Thus, the Center continues to support Tibetans studying and working in the East. In the last four years, a total of over
$30,000 has been contributed for Tibetan relief, immigration, travel and
support.

The Center has also arranged a Pen-Friend Program. Americans are now
corresponding with over 300 lamas in India or nearby countries and sending
them support of $10–20 per month. Anyone interested in establishing such a
relationship should contact TNMC, as there is always a waiting list of

Tibetans in need of help. Some people have been doing this for five years now and have established many warm and interesting friendships with Tibetans.

Several American friends have also traveled to India to help arrange for the immigration of lamas. However, expenses for bringing lamas here to visit or stay permanently is considerably more than air fare. Medical care is another major expense as many lamas are in poor physical condition from the climate and living conditions in India which are vastly different from Tibet. Legal fees and immigration are also often quite costly. For example, during a nine-month period, the total cost of making arrangements and providing for the visits of three lamas was over $10,000. But such expenses are necessary if we are to bring lamas here to help teach and transmit this tradition. Whether through such travel arrangements or by supporting these Tibetan lamas in India, we wish to help them in any way we can and will appreciate your interest. ✤

# A Survey of Center Students

*Just as a craftsman heats fine gold in the fire,*
*and the more he does so the purer, cleaner, and more*
*useful it becomes, so a Bodhisattva's foundations*
*of the good and wholesome on the first level become*
*very pure, bright, and useful for all kinds of activity.*

DAŚABHŪMIKASŪTRA

WHAT KIND OF people study Tibetan Buddhism? Why did they come and what made them stay? These questions and others are common to those interested in the Center. Only in the last ten or twenty years have Eastern systems of philosophy, psychology and meditation become current in the West, yet interest in them has been quite extensive.

To answer some of these questions, the Tibetan Nyingma Meditation Center conducted a survey of students at the Center in the winter of 1973. With the help of a psychologist, a questionnaire was devised and the responses of 72 students (approximately two-thirds of the practicing students) were recorded. The survey asked both general and personal questions, involving:

- Background data: sex, age, childhood residence, parental income and stability, education, marital status, and length of time as a practicing student.
- Interest in other spiritual paths
- Extent of travel
- Use of drugs
- Use of other methods of psychotherapy
- Interest and involvement in social or political action

- Personal background experience
- Meaningful experiences
- Results of participation at the Center

The students taking the survey were 'practicing students' at the Center. This means that, through personal interviews with Rinpoche and a willingness to commit themselves to this path, all had been accepted as members of the Center. Everyone attended classes with Rinpoche which lasted several hours once a week, and after a certain time came to evening ceremonies, which are held four times a month. Each student had periodic private interviews with the lama during which they were given specific 'practices' to perform on their own.

Perhaps the distinguishing characteristic of Center students, as opposed to seminar participants and Institute students, was that they worked on the five practices of the *Bum Nga*, the introductory practices required of lamas in Tibet. Each of these must be done 100,000 times and thus requires considerable time and effort. After completion of the *Bum Nga*, most of these students intend to go into retreat for lengthy periods and work on advanced meditation practices.

*Background data.* The survey represented many (65%) of the immediate students of Tarthang Tulku, most of whom had been students for over a year. Thirty-one percent came from upper middle class families (with an income of over $20,000 per year), and over 70% came from unbroken homes. Sixty percent of the students were males, and most students were single, in their middle twenties to early thirties. One-third of the students were married, 21% were divorced, and 26% had lived in communal environments. Three-fourths of the students had finished college, and one-fourth had advanced degrees.

*Interest.* Most of the students were led to study at the Center by reading books, through conversations with friends, and finally, by meeting Rinpoche—either by attending a seminar or through a private interview. Upon arrival, their goals included serious personal growth, quest for self-knowledge, and acquisition of meditation skills. Some mentioned a desire to find happiness, wisdom, 'enlightenment,' personal stability, and improved personal relationships.

Before coming to the Center, most students had tried a variety of spiritual paths. Childhood religious experiences ranged from deeply religious Catholics, Jews and Protestants (30%) to others with no significant religious participation. Many students (45%) had been involved in Christianity, 34% had practiced a form of yoga, 26% practiced Zen Buddhism, and 16% had used Transcendental Meditation. Another 20% had investigated other 'spiritual' paths, including Judaism, Rosicrucianism, studies on Gurdjieff, Scientology,

Aikido, Tai Chi, and other Eastern disciplines such as Sufism. Only 6% had not tried another spiritual path.

*Extent of travel.* In the last ten years, increasing numbers of American young have traveled abroad. We classified the amount of travel into three categories:

'Young, far and long' comprised those under 23 who traveled over 2000 miles for over six months–41%. 'Medium' indicated travel for over one month, generally overseas–40%. Only 16% of the students indicated having little or no travel experience in their life. Thus, many had been to other major continents.

*Use of drugs.* Another major area of investigation in this generation has been drugs. Of our group, over 90% had tried marijuana, and 70% had used LSD. A few had tried everything. It is interesting to note that at the time of the survey all use of drugs, except for occasional beer or wine, had stopped.

*Use of other methods of psychotherapy.* Many students had also been attracted to modern methods of growth and therapy. 'Growth methods' mentioned were: Gestalt, psychodrama, and various encounter groups, Rolfing, Bioenergetics, Synanon, and Human Potential. These methods attracted 33% of the students, most of whom (79%) felt them to be of some value. Forty percent of the group had used 'individual therapy,' including psychoanalysis and Gestalt, and half found some value in this approach.

*Social or political action.* Two-thirds of the students had been seriously involved in efforts to improve society: 28% in community projects, such as day care, fair housing, and aid to the handicapped; 49% in the peace movement; and 39% in more or less radical political activity.

*Personal background experience.* Answers to subjective questions are more difficult to analyze, but 27% expressed having felt a general dissatisfaction and alienation, 20% mentioned having had an unhappy or strained family life, and 26% mentioned tragedies involving friends or relatives. Few (under 10%) mentioned painful drug experiences, difficulties in their social life, or serious personal problems. On the other hand, 55% felt they had adequately happy childhood experiences, and 38% mentioned being part of a warm accepting family.

*Meaningful experiences.* The positive interests that people mentioned as meaningful in their lives included useful drug experiences (25%), prayer and meditation (16%), being in nature (15%), and music, dance and art (11%). Half of the students mentioned a definite experience of unity or empathy with others which had a positive effect on their lives.

*Results of participation at the Center.* Students at the Center were most frequently involved in a combination of individual daily practices, including formless meditation, visualization, an active exploration of the nature of the emotions, concentration exercises, group meditation, and discussions with Tarthang Tulku. Most students were also attending Tibetan ceremonies and actively studying Buddhism.

When asked to compare the effectiveness of various methods of growth, students emphasized the various insights and strengths of Nyingma techniques. The feeling behind the answers indicated that Nyingma methods brought about deep changes in one's entire life style and helped to solve problems where other therapies had been less effective.

According to students, Nyingma methods were practical, direct and insightful, and used sophisticated but clear theory to evoke self-help in all areas of their development. In general, the teachings applied usefully to all aspects of daily functioning in the world. In addition, the person and the role of the lama were considered most important, both for guidance and as an example.

In general, students emphasized more positive, open and aware attitudes. They felt more calm, yet also more active and adaptable. There was a clear tendency for many to drop a 'hippie' life-style and to become actively involved in work emphasizing self-sufficiency. They described their lives as less extreme, simpler, with fewer crises, and less involved with fantasy.

*Summary.* Without a proper control group for these questions, it is difficult to determine how much personal change was due to Nyingma practices, and how much was due to natural maturation and increased experience. In certain areas, however—optimism, pessimism, health-sickness, organization-disorganization, extreme behavior, happy-unhappy, energetic-lazy—the students' sensitivity to their own personal growth and change was quite significant. Yet this did not imply that students were able to ignore or discount negative experiences in life, but rather seemed more capable of dealing with new experiences.

As a whole, the survey presented an interesting picture: a group of widely-experienced people searching for helpful techniques, who were open to new ideas, and who, through curiosity or a deep search for meaning in life, found Tibetan Buddhism. Despite the rigor of some of the practices, and the time and energy required to perform them properly, most of those in the survey have stayed and grown in their involvement. ❖

# Dharma Publishing

*The cause of confusion and frustration in life*
*Is the virulent passion of the mind.*
*Distortion and dispersion, the causes of passion,*
*Must be replaced by incisive attentiveness.*

LAMA MI-PHAM

FOR WELL OVER a thousand years, Tibetan teachers engaged in an extensive investigation of human consciousness. Today there are many parallels between current developments in psychological theory and therapy and the Nyingma teachings. This investigation of mental processes, states of consciousness and psychological therapy, is both complex and complete. The goal of Dharma Publishing is to help make this knowledge accessible to Westerners.

Until lately, the obstacles of language and culture have blocked all access to the many methods of the Vajrayana. Combined with individualized instruction, this knowledge is gradually being communicated through translations and original works in English. Many of these texts are of special interest to psychologists and therapists, for the Nyingma offers a broad spectrum of practices which can be used effectively in any life situation.

Dharma Publishing produces and distributes books and art reproductions in the related fields of Buddhism, Tibetan art and literature, analytic philosophy and experiential psychology. A non-profit corporation, Dharma Publishing is the result of many individuals and students working closely with Rinpoche. This process has encouraged a new period of growth and expansion.

Since the vehicle reflects the meaning, Dharma Publishing also maintains technologically complete manufacturing facilities, including typesetting, production, printing and binding.

Publications fall into several broad categories. In addition to the Center's annual journal, *Crystal Mirror*, we also publish a quarterly journal, *Gesar*, which presents selections from Tibetan literature, reproductions of woodblock prints, tankas and rupas, as well as biographies of teachers in the Nyingma lineage, translations from meditation texts, and relevant articles on Buddhist philosophy and psychology. Subscriptions to *Gesar* are available for $3.50 a year.

Secondly, Dharma Publishing makes available books and reproductions of Tibetan tantric art. The archetypal motifs and subtle insight found in Tibetan tankas, mandalas and sculpture are another means of gaining knowledge of the human psyche. So far, we have produced 25 full-color tanka reproductions, and have recently reprinted the *Sacred Art of Tibet*. This book contains 44 black-and-white prints and serves as an introduction to these forms. Within this year a large definitive cloth-bound edition on Tibetan Art will be completed.

The NYINGMA PSYCHOLOGY SERIES presents works on Nyingma theory and practice. *Calm and Clear*, a translation of a meditation instruction text written in the 19th century by a Nyingma teacher, Lama Mi-pham, was the first of this series. Last summer the *Legend of the Great Stupa* was published. It presents a fascinating tale and prophecy of Tibet's past, present and future written in allegorical language. This book also includes the symbolic life story of Guru Padma Sambhava, founder of the Nyingma school. A new book is being prepared which deals specifically with Nyingma theory and practice as it relates to Western psychology.

In addition, Dharma Publishing invites articles and longer works from scholars, professionals, scientists, therapists, and others. These works can provide a broad theoretical and practical guide to the Vajrayana as each is understood and assimilated. ✤

# Suggested Reading

CHANG, GARMA C. C. (trans.). *The Hundred Thousand Songs of Milarepa.* New York: Harper, 1970.

CONZE, EDWARD. *Buddhist Thought in India.* Ann Arbor: Univ. of Michigan, 1967.

sGAMPOPA. *The Jewel Ornament of Liberation.* Translated and annotated by H. V. Guenther. Berkeley: Shambhala, 1971.

GUENTHER, H. V. *Buddhist Philosophy in Theory and Practice.* Baltimore: Pelican, 1972.

GUENTHER, H. V. (ed. and trans.). *The Life and Teachings of Naropa.* New York: Oxford, 1963.

GUENTHER, H. V. *The Royal Song of Saraha.* Berkeley: Shambhala, 1973.

GUENTHER, H. V. *The Tantric View of Life.* Berkeley: Shambhala, 1973.

GUENTHER, H. V. *Treasures on the Tibetan Middle Way.* Berkeley: Shambhala, 1969.

MI-PHAM, LAMA. *Calm and Clear.* Edited by the Tibetan Nyingma Meditation Center. Berkeley: Dharma, 1973.

MURTI, T. R. V. *The Central Philosophy of Buddhism.* London: Allen & Unwin, 1970.

PADMA SAMBHAVA. *The Legend of the Great Stupa* and *The Life Story of the Lotus Born Guru.* Berkeley: Dharma, 1973.

SHANTIDEVA. *Entering the Path of Enlightenment: Bodhicaryatara.* Translated by Marion L. Matics. New York: Macmillan, 1970.

STCHERBATSKY, TH. *Buddhist Logic.* Two volumes. New York: Dover, 1962.

STCHERBATSKY, TH. *The Conception of Buddhist Nirvana.* The Hague: Mouton, 1970.

STEIN, R. A. *Tibetan Civilization.* Stanford, Cal.: Stanford Univ. Press, 1972.

STRENG, FREDERICK. *Emptiness—A Study in Religious Meaning.* Nashville: Abingdon, 1967. ❖